100 WAYS TO IMPROVE YOUR HORSE'S BEHAVIOUR

SUSAN McBANE

David and Charles

TO SUZIE, for being one of those dogs of a lifetime, and JESS, her successor, who is beating her very own, very individual path through life.

A DAVID & CHARLES BOOK
Copyright © David & Charles Limited 2005, 2007

David & Charles is an F+W Publications Inc. company
4700 East Galbraith Road
Cincinnati, OH 45236

First published in hardback in the UK in 2005
First published in paperback in the UK in 2007
Reprinted 2008

Text copyright © Susan McBane 2005, 2007

A catalogue record for this book is available from the British Library.

ISBN-13: 978-0-7153-2029-7 hardback
ISBN-10: 0-7153-2029-7 hardback

ISBN-13: 978-0-7153-2791-3 paperback
ISBN-10: 0-7153-2791-7 paperback

Printed in China by SNP Leefung
for David & Charles
Brunel House, Newton Abbot, Devon

Commissioning Editor: Jane Trollope
Art Editor: Sue Cleave
Project Editor: Anne Plume
Production Controller: Beverley Richardson

Visit our website at www.davidandcharles.co.uk

David & Charles books are available from all good bookshops; alternatively you can contact our Orderline on 0870 9908222 or write to us at FREEPOST EX2 110, D&C Direct, Newton Abbot, TQ12 4ZZ (no stamp required UK only); US customers call 800-289-0963 and Canadian customers call 800-840-5220.

Contents

Setting yourself up for success

The topic of equine behaviour has become of more and more interest over the past twenty years or so, but especially over the last decade. Many people who wish to understand it find some books on the subject heavy going, and those without a scientific view of behaviour find them positively inaccessible. I have, therefore, purposely made this book very practical in an effort to make it helpful and encouraging. There is a Further Reading list on page 150.

The horse's world

Even today there is much unsympathetic training, not all of it created by lack of knowledge, and much caused by treating horses in ways that are not suited to the type of animal they are. Horses are social, space-loving, trickle-feeding flight animals – but they are usually managed like solitary animals who live in a den or a lair, who eat 'main meals' in the same way that we do, and who hide when scared.

How did we get it so wrong? Simply by not really thinking through the type of animal that the horse is, and giving him the management he needs. Early domesticators of horses probably did not care about the animals' welfare, but only about their own convenience, a situation that, sadly, still exists in some quarters, and so inappropriate practices have largely continued. We have given both parties a massive handicap that causes considerable problems all round.

Horses are extremely sensitive animals who perceive the world rather differently from us. Their eyesight is probably the sense that is the least like ours: they seem to see colour differently from us, and their range of perception is not bounded by a circle shape in front of them, but is a narrow streak of sharp vision almost all around them, and into which they have to focus by moving the head up and down. Their hearing is wider in range than ours; their sense of smell is formidable; their sense of taste tends towards liking sweet foods; and their sense of touch is most like ours. They love firm stroking (social grooming), but are terrified of, and angered by pain, so it has no place in the management regime of a good horseman.

The flight instinct

Horses are prey animals, and their first defence when frightened is flight, appearing as anything from a tiny shy to a headlong bolt. This instinct is what we try in all our training to suppress. It is the main reason why anyone dealing with

4

horses must try to be calm and quiet, firm, positive, fair and consistent so that horses feel safe and content with us. Uptight, weak and especially sharp or brutal people have no place around animals like this.

How horses deal with stress

If horses do not feel safe and content, they become frightened and stressed, and they show this in various ways, not all of them recognized as 'vices' or stereotypies, aberrant behaviour or abnormal, unnatural behaviour patterns – but that is what these behaviours are. They are outlets for distress in circumstances where horses cannot run away, and are habits that give them some relief from their circumstances.

It is now acknowledged by the best horse managers, behavioural scientists and sensitive horse people that it is wrong to physically stop a horse performing a stereotypical activity, as this

denies him the outlet it provides. The key is to improve the management so that he does not feel the need to perform them. Some habits, however, become so ingrained that we just have to try to lessen them by good treatment.

Pain

Pain and even significant discomfort are not borne well by horses in general. They show it by working poorly or refusing, by dangerous or defensive behaviour during work, by becoming withdrawn, by patchy sweating, a dull coat, lack of interest in life and sunken eyes, backward-pointing ears, and nostrils wrinkled up and back.

It is crucial to ensure that the horse's tack or harness fits him, and it is essential to keep checking this, as he changes shape during his yearly cycle and in the course of his muscular development. Back, teeth and feet are common sites of discomfort and pain, but physical injury or disease of any part of the body can cause pain.

Becoming a pair with your horse

As herd animals, horses look to their peers for protection and mutual comfort. As part of the horse's world, we must try to become seen by the horse in that light: he will not respect weak, inconsistent, untrustworthy or cruel humans.

When you are with your horse, keep calm and quiet, radiate caring about him, be self-confident and 'in control' in your demeanour, be patient but insistent in your (reasonable) requests, and he will come to respect you and look to you for protection and guidance. Study your horse, and generally learn all you can so that you come to know him and can tell whether you are being advised well or badly. You will realize, one day, that you are the most important person in your horse's life. It is a real compliment when he leaves his friends and comes to you out of choice, not for food, but because he wants to be with you.

5

Stable stress

Horse management

Many researchers and scientists in the field of equine behaviour are now convinced that behaviour problems in horses stem largely from management that is inappropriate for the species. In this context it is unfortunate for horses that as a species they are very adaptable, a characteristic that could well have persuaded many of those people who use and manage them to believe that the system of stabling as most of us know it is perfectly acceptable. In many countries it is quite usual to keep horses in some sort of housing, and stalls (tie-stalls) and loose boxes (box stalls) have been in use for thousands of years – even though it is patently obvious that confining them in this way is the exact opposite to how horses live naturally.

Signs of distress are not always clear to everyone, but will appear in discussion throughout this book. They are evident in the behavioural habits formerly called vices (as if the horse were doing wrong), but now more correctly known as stereotypies, such as crib-biting, wind-sucking, weaving and boxwalking; distress is also evident in actions performed frequently or habitually, such as kicking the walls and door, excessive pawing, head-twirling and tossing, scraping the teeth on ledges, the manger, the walls or door, tongue lolling, rug-tearing, fence-pacing, self-mutilation, and various other behaviours that horses would not normally indulge in, if they led a natural life. There are also natural, normal equine actions such as wood chewing, calling out, biting, striking out and kicking, any of which they might do in natural circumstances and in normal interaction with others.

It is now largely believed that these, and some other stereotypies, are a result not so much of boredom (which traditionally was always given as the reason), but of the mental and physical frustration, tension, agitation and distress caused by inappropriate management. This might include confinement, inadequate social contact with other horses, insufficient fibre or roughage in the diet, high points of the day such as feeding, radios constantly playing, excessive concentrate rations, rough grooming, inadequate exercise in amount and type, lack of liberty and space, unsuitable clothing regimes, being obliged to stay in a stable near unfriendly horses, separation from friends, unnaturally early weaning, stressful work in type and amount, poor training and riding or driving techniques, and even non-straw bedding. That's quite a list already – and I could go on!

There is a great deal that we *can* do, however, so as to give horses a more horse-friendly environment, particularly if we have control over our facilities. Even in livery yards, the more clients, both long-term and potential, who push for better facilities – and keep on doing so – the more likely they are to be realized.

1 Make your stables and yard horse-friendly

Can any stabling or confinement situation be horse-friendly? Domestic horses still have the urge to roam unrestricted, mainly at a slow walk, eating as they go, with friends and family all around for security and protection. This is not how most domestic horses are kept, of course. Can a compromise be reached? Yes!

What do horses want?

Basically, horses want to be both mentally and physically comfortable. That's all: but within that brief answer are a great many considerations. So, what do they need in order to be mentally and physically comfortable, and how can we provide it? On a basic management level, horses want food, water, shelter, company, space and movement.

There can be no doubt that the majority of horses do not, in fact, want to live the sort of 'natural' life often meted out to them, in a featureless, exposed field, with bad drainage, restricted, over-rich or boring grazing, exposed to insects and the elements, with nowhere dry, sheltered and comfortable to lie and rest, and no space to run away from bosses or bullies. Equally, few want to be confined almost permanently within four walls with no freedom, the victim of an erratic supply of food and water, uncomfortable clothing, surrounded by their own urine and droppings and unable to interact naturally with other inmates. Finally they will, most importantly, want to be free from discomfort and pain.

What can I do?

Ideally, domestic horses would be on a group management system where they are loose together in compatible groups in large barns with enclosures and paddocks. This is impossible for most owners, but we should still aim for the best possible compromise.

- First, make sure that you only put horses that are friendly to each other in adjacent stables, otherwise their stress levels will rise. Horses love a view, so try to give them a large loosebox with a minimum of two outlets. Also, they should be allowed at least to sniff and touch their (friendly) neighbours through the bars of their partitions, or ideally to mutual groom over partition walls that are no higher than their withers.

- Use clean straw bedding (chopped or otherwise), as horses love and *need* to rootle about, and behavioural problems seem to be more common on non-straw bedding. Try to adopt full daily mucking out. If you use rubber matting, keep a half bed on it, as horses need a soft, absorbent surface on which to stale, and to lie down.

- Keep feeding, fibre and watering points low, ideally at ground level, and provide simultaneously as many different fibre choices as you can, so as to mimic nature – hay, haylage, different short-chopped forages, and so on.

- Create pens outside the stables (front and back if possible) into which the horses can wander at will, socialize and feel less confined. (In wet weather, use waterproof rugs, if necessary.)

2 Install mirrors in stables

Work undertaken at the University of Lincoln in the UK has shown that horses manifesting stereotypical behaviour such as weaving followed these habits much less frequently if they had mirrors installed in their stables. Although they must know that it is not another horse, it would be most interesting to know if they recognize themselves.

What is the point of mirrors?

Mirrors are valuable devices for bringing light and apparent space into an area, and they certainly have this effect in stables; but most noticeable is the horse's reaction, because most will go and stand quietly next to them, even when they can see other horses stabled next door or nearby. Anything that has a calming effect on a horse, and which he enjoys, must be good, because if the horse becomes calmer, he is happier and more content, and this is what all good horsemasters aim to achieve in their horses.

What do I need to consider?

The mirrors used must, of course, be shatter-proof, and there are various plastic-type materials that are generally used for stables; these are available from various sources in different countries, and are sometimes advertised in the equestrian press. National equestrian trade associations should be able to put you in touch with a suitable supplier. Putting up mirror tiles does not seem to work, and can even upset horses, as the image is fragmented by the tile edges.

To best advantage the mirrors should be fairly large, and cover, say, half the wall above the kicking boards

of a stable. The horse certainly seems to need to see the reflection as if it were another horse next door, so the head and upper half of the body need to be clearly seen in an uninterrupted image. Obviously any mirror needs to be securely fixed; and they work best, it seems, when they are kept clean!

Different locations within the stable can be tried, to see which the horse seems to prefer. Siting the mirror opposite the door to bring in light and a view had an agitating effect on an

acquaintance's horse (an inveterate weaver), but he calmed down when it was placed on an end wall, and came to love it. He was also able to sniff his neighbour (a friend) over his partition wall, but often stood by his mirror in preference.

Introduce your horse carefully to the mirror, talking to him and stroking him, but stay outside his stable until you are sure of his reaction. However, most horses, it seems, take to them very quickly.

3 Introduce stable toys

When stable toys were first marketed a few years ago, many people laughed at the thought. But in practice, they have helped many stabled horses find something entertaining to do during their long hours of confinement. There's nothing new about toys or devices for entertainment: many old books suggest them, and a few are described below.

Does a horse really need toys, and will he play with them?

A horse could well be helped psychologically by toys, either the commercially available sort or simpler, home-made ones. They act as valuable occupational therapy for highly strung horses, and help to fill out idle hours when horses may have no hay left and have nothing to do. They can also help prevent the development of stereotypical behaviour. Horses do play with them, but only some of them some of the time, depending on the horse's inclinations.

What can I do?

- One of the oldest and most popular things to do is to give your horse a log (they like damp ones) and some tree or shrub branches, ideally with leaves, to chew and play with in his stable. Chewing wood and branches is perfectly natural and normal: any non-poisonous and non-prickly species will do. The log can be left on the floor for him to chomp up, and branches can be tied in a bundle and hung in a corner of the box or stuffed in a hay-rack.
- Another old tactic was to leave the horse's own straw or hay wisp in his box or manger, and let him dismantle and eat it at will. A sod of turf in the manger will also keep him entertained.
- You can also try filling a plastic bottle with water and hanging it slightly away from a corner so that the horse can push it around, but not constantly bump into it.
- A variety of salt and flavoured mineral licks can also be supplied, and a horse of mine used to like throwing around old numnahs and kicking a plastic football about in his box.
- Commercial toys sell readily, and include stacks of licks on a rope; large, blow-up balls with handles for horses to play with in their stable or paddock; and barrel-shaped feeders with holes that deliver nuts as the horse noses them around (on an area not bedded down).

4 Make a horsey playpen

In situations where grazing turnout is limited or non-existent, a playpen can truly be a boon for horses that would otherwise be stabled for many hours. Some yards do turn out their horses in a manège (ideally with hay or haylage), but in the absence of pasture, a dedicated area for horse recreation allows a much greater opportunity for socializing and activity.

What sort of facility are we looking at?

Liberty, even in a pen, has a great balancing and calming effect on horses, and this will show in their wellbeing, demeanour and behaviour. The bigger the pen the better, but anything is better than nothing. Anything you can think of to entertain horses and keep them occupied, not only eating, is a big advantage when turnout is scarce. On mainland Europe such facilities are not unusual, and horses live in them perfectly contentedly.

Furthermore, the facilities in such a pen, given that it is a reasonable size, should be arranged so that not everything is available in one area. Apart from this causing possible congestion, if they are spread about it encourages the horses to move around and exercise themselves at a gentle walk, as they do most of the time in natural conditions.

Mention has already been made about constructing pens outside the stables so that horses can wander in and out, and with a little thought and imagination a larger, separate area can be dedicated to horse recreation. Pens of varying sizes can be made in most yards – I've never yet come across a yard with absolutely no spare space whatsoever – and all those yard proprietors who have introduced them say that they are a big advantage, and that the horses love them.

Ideally the surface should be of earth or something similar, and

depending on size, several different functional areas can be designated to encourage the horses to exercise. A common excuse for not turning horses out on a manège is that they just stand and do nothing, or start chewing the rails, fence-walking and even weaving. Of course they *will* do this if they have nothing to do once they've had a buck and a kick, so putting hay or haylage out in nets is the minimal facility that should be offered on a manège. Horses in nature spend a limited amount of time sleeping and resting, and all the rest of it eating (two-thirds of their time) and socializing with each other.

In a pen, friendly horses can be turned out in twos or more, depending on the area. The fencing can be made of permanent posts and rails or wire, or portable, flexible rail fencing can be used. Electrified tape can be used, if necessary. There can be a shelter area, an area for hay, or haynets can be hung around the fencing (at least one more net than horses). Carrots and other roots can be scattered all over the ground area for horses to forage on – though not on the rolling and resting areas.

If the fencing can be arranged to take in a tree or a shrub or two, the horses will appreciate them very much. An undulating area is also more interesting, and slightly more physically taxing than a flat one; but this depends on the area available.

A sand area within the pen is a very inviting spot for horses to roll on and dig up, and keeps them cleaner

than mud; and an area under cover can be bedded down so horses that are out for a long time can use it for resting and lying down.

This sort of facility can either be a separate one, or it can be built outside a free-entry barn so that horses can be kept in a compatible group and have shelter, somewhere clean and dry to rest inside, a sand rolling area outside, eating facilities (fibre) inside and out but not too near the resting area; also large 'brush stations' can be set up, as used for cattle, so they can scrub and rub themselves as they would on trees and shrubs in nature. A very popular facility in practice!

If there is a covered area offering shelter from wind and rain, private owners can leave their horses in such a pen all day whilst they are at work. In livery yards, if several clients ask for this sort of facility (and it really need not be expensive) most sensible yard proprietors will be willing to devise something along these lines, for the sake of good business, at least! Everyone can get together to help construction and so speed up the process, for the benefit of the horses.

5 Make your forage last longer

Probably most people are tired of hearing and reading that horses in nature eat for about two-thirds of their twenty-four hours. Well, that's the way it is. Domestic horses at grass also eat for that long, whether or not the grass is quite suitable for them; but stabled horses have often eaten through their forage rations in half that time, or even less.

Does that matter?

Forage is a horse's 'life blood' when it comes to eating. They are biologically programmed to eat for most of the time, and therefore they have an inborn need to chew, a trait that we have to live with. I can never understand why it bothers some people that horses are always wanting to eat, when it is their nature. The two things they were designed to do best are to run and to eat. Unlike people, cats and dogs, they don't sleep for hours on end or automatically want to sleep when they have eaten. Therefore, if they have finished their forage, they have nothing to do – and that creates trouble.

What can I do?

- The first thing to do is to make sure that your horse has forage of the right energy level and nutrient content for his constitution (poor doer/good doer) and his work; but you also need to take into account the type of grazing he has. Rich grass could mean he needs low-energy forage, and vice versa. This way, you can feed enough forage to keep him occupied for as long as is necessary, without creating too much energy or giving him a hay belly.
- Once that's decided, work out ways of providing the forage so that he cannot take too much at once. There are, of course, small-hole nets that oblige the horse to fiddle out a few strands of hay at a time.

- Another ruse is to use hayracks with a lid, made out of metal bars or wires in squares, and once again, these oblige the horse to take small amounts; and there are large hay mangers with lids with slats in them, which slide down as they empty. Again, the horse can only get small amounts at a time.
- Finally, short-chopped forage takes longer to eat than long forage, so leave your horse large tubs of a suitable type for him to nibble at.
- It has been found that horses eat for longer when given two or more different types of forage all the time, and when they can eat from a low level. Tubs and floor mangers in each corner are the answer.

6 Consider a stable companion

Horses evolved to live with company: in the wild, any horse on its own – a lone stallion, or the occasional lone female – would soon succumb to predators. Stallions form bachelor bands, and females, too, group together or try to latch on to another herd for the company, security and protection that herd life offers. But stabled horses cannot do this …

Won't another animal in the stable create problems?

Horses and ponies that are deprived of close company with another horse often form firm friendships with other animals. Racing history, for example, is full of stories of famous racehorses (who are usually entires, of course) who had a sheep, goat or cat or, in a couple of cases I remember, a cockerel or hen for company. Sometimes these creatures travelled to the racecourse with their horse. Small ponies have formed ideal companions for such horses, remembering that traditionally racehorses enjoy bigger loose boxes than most other horses.

If you can arrange for your horse to have a large stable or perhaps a makeshift box made out of a pen with sliprails in another building (but with a view out), there is no reason why two animals could not live together. Of course, you will have to be sure that they do actually like each other. Some horses are frightened of, or even dislike animals of other species, but if you can see that a friendship is forming, try them together by all means.

I often feel sorry for stallions, who normally live very lonely, artificial lives in the society we have created for horses. They are ideal candidates for a stable companion, as is any horse that has to live alone – hardly *ever* a good idea for horses, though there are a very few exceptions.

People generally worry about trouble arising when the horse or pony is required to leave his companion and go out and work. This is not a problem as long as the owner and horse have a strong, mutually respectful relationship; it only causes trouble when the horse does not have much regard for the human. It is the same situation as asking a horse to leave its herdmates in the field, or a friend living next door: if the horse kicks up a significant fuss, this may be construed as bad behaviour and it is the fault of the human, who has failed to instil respect, and not the horse.

7 Making compulsory box rest bearable

The notion of 'box rest' has a really depressing effect on most caring horse owners. Even if a horse is injured and in pain, most of them must surely hate being confined to their boxes, their normal turnout and exercise routine turned upside down, going stir crazy whilst other horses go out. Can box rest really be made bearable?

The real meaning of box rest

A while ago I was talking to someone whose vet had prescribed three weeks' box rest for her horse. She finished her chores whilst we chatted, then put a headcollar on the horse, opened the stable door and made to lead him out. 'What are you doing?' I asked. She looked surprised. 'I'm turning him out because he can't be ridden,' she replied. 'He can't stay in here for three weeks.' I explained exactly what box rest meant, and why it was necessary, but she still took the horse to his field where he had a great time tearing around with his friends. The result was not unexpected!

Box rest means exactly that – rest *in the box* and nowhere else, unless the vet or physiotherapist has prescribed, say, short walks in hand (which could be combined with grazing) as part of a treatment/rehabilitation programme. In some cases the horse may have to be cross-tied because he is not even allowed to lie down or move about for a given length of time.

The bad news is that box rest can range from a day or two, to several months, depending on the injury. The good news is that, given thoughtful management, most horses tolerate it surprisingly well. The time normally spent exercising will be taken up in extra management and care jobs. However, if you cannot be available for your horse frequently throughout his day, some other responsible and trustworthy person (or people) will have to attend to him, or his mental state will certainly suffer.

How can I help?

From a practical management point of view, scrupulous attention must be paid to the bed, removing droppings *and*

- Spend time carefully grooming him; damp spongeing his eyes, nostrils and muzzle, and between his legs (sheath or udder) and under the tail will refresh him.
- Try giving him a gentle massage, maybe with calming aromatherapy oils such as lavender or chamomile. Other bodywork techniques such as shiatsu and Tellington Touch can certainly help, both of which you can perform yourself if you read up on them and carry them out sensitively and in an unhurried way.
- Depending on the reason he is confined, gentle stretches will help to keep him supple. All these techniques will help keep his body loosened and toned up, and will make him feel better.
- Change his rugs frequently (these must be as light and comfortable as possible), and keep them aired, dry and clean. Be very sure that he really *needs* clothing before you use it.
- Flower remedies to induce calmness, placed inside his bottom lip, in his water, or on a cut apple, could help, as could a herbal supplement for the same purpose, and also homoeopathic remedies.

Seeing to his mental and physical needs will help him to feel wanted and loved, during a period that has the potential to be a very trying time for him.

wet bedding several times a day, and to picking out the feet three or four times a day. The bed really must be kept clean and *dry*: when a bed is damp it is damp with urine, not water, which is bad for hoof horn, and it also contaminates the stable's airspace, and is therefore bad for the horse's lungs. Full mucking out is best, but taking care to raise as little dust as possible. Diet may be advised by the vet, but *ad lib* hay is usual for most horses, and tubs of short-chopped forages; and it is especially important to provide enough to keep the horse satisfied overnight, which is when many horses run out of fibre; you should check this, last thing.

In addition, the following strategies will almost certainly make him feel more comfortable:

- Give several very small feeds of whatever else he has to have. Also take in carrots, apples and other succulents frequently, and pull or cut grass – armfuls of it – for your horse.
- Twigs and branches with leaves are also appreciated.
- Provide stable toys.
- Keep the water container full, and make sure it is refilled with fresh water, not merely topped up.
- Probably most important of all, make sure the horse has company, either another horse or pony always nearby, perhaps in the yard and able to talk to him over the door, or another animal he is fond of. Even you yourself, sitting in his box reading a book, is company for him.

8 Learn special care for a claustrophobic horse

Opinions vary as to whether or not horses are actually claustrophobic in general, or whether the condition affects only individual horses. My experience is that there are certainly some horses and ponies that cannot tolerate being in an enclosed space even for short periods, whether a stable, a trailer or horsebox, and even, occasionally, a small paddock.

What causes claustrophobia in horses?

It is not surprising that some horses are claustrophobic (as are some people) because, by evolution, they are plains animals. Although the very early horse ancestors were woodland animals with traits that have come down to some horses today, the species' most recent evolution was in open spaces.

Confinement involving most of the horse's time is unreasonable and may be expected to cause any horse distress; however, some appear unable to tolerate even short periods in the confines of a stable, a trailer or horsebox, or any kind of small turnout or holding area. Some, despite sympathetic training, cannot bear to be tied up because of the restriction, and some more extreme cases do not like passing through any area where they feel enclosed, such as a tunnel or dense woodland.

How can I help?

Clearly, the ideal life for a horse or pony that is claustrophobic is outdoors with a roomy, light shelter, some hard standing, well-drained ground, and as large a field or paddocks as can

be found. Also the company of non-claustrophobic horses should help a little.

Whilst you are looking for, or trying to create such facilities, the following procedures may help:
- Try to obtain as large, light and airy a stable as possible with at least one viewpoint outdoors.
- Stable the horse for as little time as possible, ideally in a stable with a pen attached so that he can go in and out at will.
- Let him be out, and ideally with some grazing, in good conditions as much as possible.

- Work the horse as often as possible (within reason – two short spells daily are better than one longer one), and spend time grazing and walking him in hand if grazing facilities are poor.
- Try to keep him in a play-pen area, with shelter, when he is not stabled or grazing.
- If he has to travel, use as large a vehicle as possible, and with as many windows as possible to allow a maximum of natural light in, and a wide view out. Keep the inside painted a light colour.

9 Teach a horse to step back from the door

It is really tiresome when you open a horse's door, maybe loaded with equipment from tack to feed buckets and haynets, to find him standing resolutely in your way with no intention of moving. You struggle to get past, telling the horse to go back, but it doesn't make any difference: he doesn't budge! What's the problem?

Why should he go back, anyway?

A horse should automatically move back when people enter their stable, for reasons of safety and good manners. Specifically this is because:

- It is inconvenient and risky for a person to have to push past the horse.
- Some horses may straightaway take the opportunity to barge out, and may even knock us over.
- It is inconvenient for us to have to push him back each time we go in or out.
- It is a clear sign that the horse has insufficient respect for, or even feels he is superior to, humans, even though we have entered his personal space.

- The horse may never have been trained from youth to step back from the door when a person enters. Whatever the reason, the horse should be taught to step backwards. Ultimately, he should step back from the door without being asked, but getting him used to doing so when he hears a suitable instruction such as – logically to us – 'go back' or 'back up', is an improvement. This also makes it a simpler task to teach him to step back when he is being ridden, too.

What can I do?

Using horse body language is a simple way to do this. In herd talk, smooth contact movements such as nuzzling with the lips, tongue or teeth are pleasant-feeling actions meaning friendship (which is why it is preferable to stroke horses rather than pat them), whereas sharp, intermittent movements such as nips, bites, shoves and kicks are uncomfortable ones that usually mean 'go away, and get out of my space'.

You can mimic this by bracing your thumb straight against the side of your index finger with the fingers formed into a tight fist so that the tip of the thumb protrudes a little but is strong and supported, and then repeatedly jab the horse on the front of the shoulder or low on the chest, commanding 'back'. After a few assertive, but not rough jabs, most horses will move back – and as soon as he does it is essential to stop jabbing and say 'good boy' *instantly,* to teach him that this is what you want.

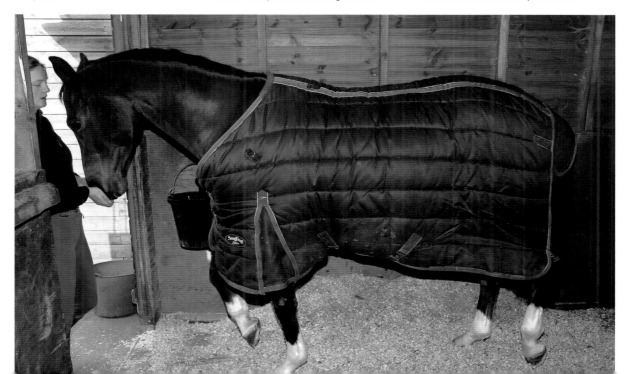

10 Control the aggressive stabled horse

Many people are afraid of aggressive horses in the stable, and wisely so. There is no doubt that some should only be dealt with by professionals, and are not really suitable to be in 'general circulation' among less knowledgeable or less experienced horse enthusiasts. If, however, you are faced with such a horse, these tips should help.

Why are some horses aggressive?

It is well known that some equine traits run in families, and heightened aggressiveness is one. Inborn aggressiveness, however, is a minority trait. Most aggressive horses have been made that way by unsuitable management for them as individuals, and often by general bad handling. There are right and wrong ways to deal with horses in general, but they are all different, and it is always important to assess each horse as an individual, because management suitable for one may not be suitable for his or her neighbour.

Aggressiveness is caused mainly by pain, fear, memory of bad treatment, frustration at needs not being met (mating for stallions, insufficient fibre, insufficient freedom, lack of company, inadequate exercise – and so on), excess energy

levels in the feed, the horse obviously considering himself superior to a person or people in general, being teased (such as knowing feed is near, but not being able to get at it) and self-defence. Inconsistent handling also causes insecurity.

It may be necessary to call in an experienced horse person or behavioural therapist to assess the horse, his history if possible, and his situation; and you may have to consider having him retrained, because whenever possible, correcting the root cause is always best. For instance, if the horse is only aggressive when tack or harness appears, he obviously associates work with distress. If he is only aggressive towards certain people, he is either afraid or disrespectful of them. If he is aggressive all the time, though, he has deeper-seated problems. Low-level, constant pain and discomfort can certainly cause aggression, such as from badly shod feet, internal pain, unrecognized diseases and injuries such as osteoarthritis or muscle tears, uncomfortable clothing from which he cannot escape – and so on.

What can I do?

Whilst the cause of the problem and its treatment are being sorted out in the long term, the horse still has to be handled in the stable on a daily basis, so certain safety techniques should become habitual to his handlers.

- Firstly, it is essential that the handlers always maintain a confident, quiet and firm attitude around the horse. The type of person who teases horses, pokes at them, hurts them or in other ways 'gets their own back' should be kept away from such horses (or any animals, in fact) as such treatment will make them worse. However, so will fearfulness, pussy-footing around and dithering.
- It is helpful if the horse always wears a strong, well-fitting, comfortable head-collar with a short (6in) catching rope dangling from the jaw ring. This enables you to catch hold of it over the door whilst you open it, clip on the leadrope and tie the horse up short enough so that he cannot turn his head round far enough to bite you as you attend to him. This will usually mean tying him with his nose about a third of a metre or a foot from the wall. To get him to come to the door initially, offer a treat and catch the short rope as you give it to him and praise him.
- When you have finished your work, untie the horse, take him to the door with you, command him to stand and hold him very near the head while you go out, then unclip the leadrope from outside as you praise him. If you let him free whilst you are in the box he may attack you.

- Always keep an eye on the horse as you work, and avoid putting yourself in a position where he can bite, kick, tread on you, or squash you against the wall. Give firm, polite commands and praise him when he complies. If he bites, always face his head when near it, if he strikes with the forelegs do not go in front of him, and if he kicks do not go behind him. Remember that some horses also cow kick. Do not either tickle or scrub at him when grooming, as any discomfort will make him worse. Put his rugs on and take them off in a considerate but no-nonsense manner. Try to put him in another box while you muck out.
- Many behavioural therapists will advise you to ignore his antics, but to praise him when he is good; others will advise you to say a stern 'no' when he shows aggression and, as always, to praise him when good. I agree with the latter advice.

11 Dealing with a horse who swings his quarters

This behaviour is surely one of the most off-putting for the handler: when you approach the horse's door, with or without tack, buckets, grooming kit or treats, round come his hindquarters, sometimes with the hind hooves threatening as well; his ears are laid flat back, he shows the white of his eye, and he has a really nasty look on his face. What's going on?

- With the stable door closed, walk confidently, but not in a rush, up to the door. If the quarters come round, say the horse's name in a friendly, self-assured manner and then maybe rustle a bag containing mints to give him, or make strange noises such as imitating horse-blowing noises

Aggression or defence?

In most cases, the horse swinging the quarters in this way is defensive behaviour – but not always. Over time, a horse has sometimes come to dislike being dealt with at all, usually because of poor handling technique; sometimes it only happens when tack appears, or a certain person, particular equipment such as a specific saddle, or when the horse knows, through other activities, that, say, he is being loaded up to go somewhere he associates with distress – generally exhaustion or pain.

Just because the horse has a nasty look on his face doesn't mean that he is aggressive: he could just be trying to keep you away as a means of defending himself. It is vital that you take careful note of just when this behaviour occurs, and to whom: if it is all the time and to everyone, the horse has big problems, and they normally stem from past unpleasantness of some kind.

What can I do?

- First of all you should really do your utmost to find out the cause and correct it, maybe with expert help; but always remember that it is no good hitting or otherwise hurting the horse on his quarters, as this will almost certainly provoke hard kicking at the door, or at anyone standing there if it is open. This is counter-productive and dangerous.

– anything to get him to turn round.
- Always have a strong well-fitting, comfortable headcollar on him with a short catching strap or rope on the jaw ring. As he turns, say 'good boy', give him a mint as a reward for good behaviour, get hold of the catching strap, and carry on as in the preceding topic, page 20.

12 Cure the rug ripper

Rug tearing is a very expensive habit! It used to be classified as a stable vice, and can be a most frustrating habit to deal with. We wrap the horse up in a rug (US: blanket) only for his own benefit, but he ungratefully rips it up! So we buy cheaper rugs to try and compromise the situation, but it doesn't cure him. What can we do?

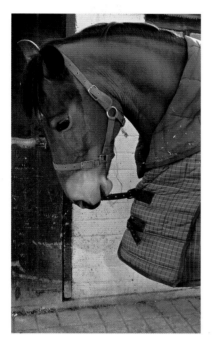

Remember that horses may wear a rug for most of their twenty-four-hour day – and most rugs do slip and create an unpleasant pull, usually on the shoulders, the withers, sometimes on the point of the hips, and maybe between the legs.

How can I help?

- Check that your rug is not tight anywhere, does not pull when the horse moves, and stays in place: a modern, well shaped rug should do all this. Make sure that the leg straps are not twisted, and that there are no bits of bedding stuck to the lining: this can really irritate a horse – both his skin and his temper!

- Do not clip your horse any more than is absolutely necessary (or at all, in many cases), and only rug him when he is genuinely cold (see page 34). Check him for sore or itchy skin either from pressure, dirt, skin disease or external parasites.

- If the problem continues, consider a job and a life for him without rugs, keep him well sheltered but not cosseted, and clip him as little as possible.

- Ensure that he has a high-fibre diet so that he stays naturally warm. High-energy forages plus sugar beet and oil are adequate for many working horses.

What is the cause of it?

Most people rug up horses too much and clip them too extensively. Horses do feel the cold, but apparently not as much as we do, and as fibre digesters they have a very efficient form of internal central heating if they are fed properly, with ample fibre rations – this is because the digestion of fibre actually creates body heat.

Most horses apparently tear up their rugs simply because they are uncomfortable. Many rugs do not fit the horse (despite being the right size) and are, therefore, uncomfortable.

13 Deal with a horse who chews everything

This is largely a problem of young horses – but not entirely. With such a horse you reach the point at which you dare not leave anything at all important within reach of those non-stop teeth, and then the horse may turn on his stable, play with his buckets, chew his rugs – and then look thoroughly miserable when you remove absolutely everything he can wreck.

Why does he do it?

Many young horses do it when they are teething, like babies and children. Some, it is felt, undoubtedly do it because they were weaned too early and deprived of the suckling action (six months old or before is really very early to separate a foal from its mother, eight months or more now being felt to be more humane). Boredom is another reason.

Lack of fibre is surely an excellent reason, too: horses have an inborn, psychological need to chew for many hours a day, eating fibrous food (grass, shrubs and trees, including bark) which is normal behaviour for horses. Insecurity and anxiety may come into it, when it can equate to 'comfort-eating' in people.

How can I help?

- Do get your vet or an equine dental technician to check your horse's teeth so that discomfort can be dealt with. Young horses may need this service every three months, and others not less than once a year, and probably more often.
- Be patient with a youngster: he will probably grow out of this habit, but meanwhile give him a log and non-poisonous shrub or tree branches in his stable to chew. Older horses, too, love them.
- It is known that horses kept on straw bedding have fewer mouth-orientated problem behaviours than

those on other bedding materials, so try a cleaned straw bedding product.
- Toys he can actually grip and chomp should help him, too.
- Make sure your horse has a generous fibre ration – hay, haylage and a variety of short-chopped forages – to keep him nourished and busy when he is in. A boring diet with the same forage all the time is unnatural, and can trigger exploration with different tastes.
- Finally, coating the surfaces he chews with lemon juice should put him off, but do not remove this outlet for him without first introducing the measures detailed above.

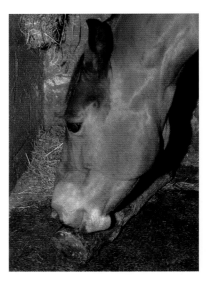

14 Stop the door kicker!

This really is an infuriating habit, particularly to people nearby. It is extremely tempting to yell 'STOPPIT!' down the yard at the horse, and the more ignorant of us will go up to the horse and actually hit him or shout at him from close quarters, only to find that as soon as our back is turned he does it again! So what's the answer?

What's the cause of it?

It is probably frustration or attention-seeking, both of which are quite understandable in conventionally managed stabled horses who find confinement for nearly all their day very hard to bear. One theory is that horses just like to hear the noise.

Apart from the maddening (to us) noise, door kicking can damage the door and injure the horse's legs due to the concussion; so we should try to stop it if at all possible.

What can I do?

- If over-confinement is the cause, clearly the answer is to get the horse out more, on grass ideally, in a suitably equipped playpen with company, being led out for interest, ridden, driven – anything that will help to while away the hours that he has to be confined.
- Ensuring that the horse has an ample fibre supply when stabled will address the immediate hunger excuse; but some horses do get bored with the same sort of forage all the time. Try to give the horse a variety of forages, as well as pulled grass if he can't be grazed.

If the cause seems to be attention-seeking, the usually recommended solution is to ignore it completely. If you approach him, even to reprimand him, he's got your attention. When the horse stops kicking, call 'good boy' to him, approach him as a reward, and maybe give him a treat if you are near enough to give it within a second or two. Bear in mind that treats given too late can make the problem worse.

15 Help a horse who crib-bites or wind-sucks

Crib-biting and wind-sucking are two of the classic four 'vices' (the other two being box-walking and weaving), the ones that everyone thinks of when you mention 'vices': and once established, they are incurable. Known as 'stereotypical [repetitive and apparently pointless] aberrant behaviour patterns', they become so ingrained that they are with the horse for life, whether he is stabled or turned out.

Crib-biting involves the horse grasping something with his teeth (a ledge or even his own knee) and apparently creating a vacuum at the back of his throat which is then released, making the familiar grunting noise. Wind-suckers do not grasp anything but simply swing their heads up and down, grunting on the downward swing.

Research indicates that only insignificant amounts of air are swallowed during this action, and it does not cause indigestion and colic. Conversely, horses are likely to crib-bite and wind-suck more *because* of the distress of indigestion, colic or gastric ulcers. A friend of mine had a competition stallion who crib-bit when on a low-fibre/high-concentrate diet, but who stopped when the diet was corrected.

Research into stereotypies has gone on for some decades, and it seems to be agreed that performing them induces in the horse the production of the body's own feel-good substances (specifically endorphins and encephalins); these reduce the feeling of stress the horse experiences under a management regime that is inappropriate for him as an individual.

Horses are all different, like people and other animals, which is why some horses crib-bite whilst others do not, but may find other releases. It is mainly, but not exclusively, highly strung, sensitive types who crib-bite and wind-suck – Arabs and Thoroughbreds, and animals with much of their blood, including some modern types of warmblood.

How do they start and what's involved?

First of all, forget what you have heard about horses copying these stereotypies from others. They don't copy them. They are also more likely to develop in young horses than older ones. If several horses on a yard begin crib-biting and wind-sucking it is not because they are copying each other, but most likely because that is their predisposition when suffering under management that is unsuitable for them.

How can I stop my horse crib-biting or wind-sucking?

The answer now is 'don't', the reason being that it is inhumane to physically deprive the horse of his chosen way of relieving his stress. Even if your horse adopted these behaviours in other ownership and your management is more appropriate to him, they may be so ingrained that he now needs the feeling they produce – he has become an endorphin junkie. That's one plausible theory, anyway.

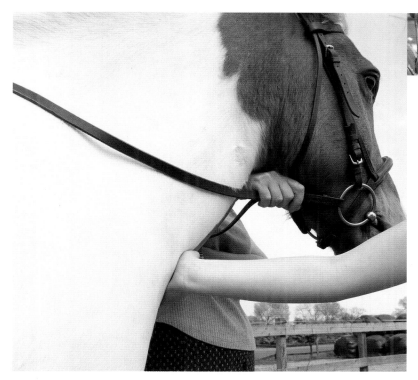

Another may be that they are firmly established, stereotypical habits that cannot now be eliminated.

The old way of 'curing' these behaviours was, and often still is, to fit the horse with a tight cribbing strap round the throat with a metal fitting that causes the horse discomfort in the throat area, or prevents him arching his neck, when he tries to crib-bite or wind-suck. These straps reduce the occurrence of these behaviours, but it seems clear that they must increase the horse's frustration and distress by causing discomfort, and by removing his chosen outlet, and so must be rejected on animal welfare grounds.

Another way to prevent crib-biting (although it won't stop wind-sucking, of course) is to remove all ledges and make the inside of the stable as smooth as possible so that the horse has nothing to get hold of. Of course, this necessitates fitting a grille to the top of his door, so making him feel even worse. Some owners even fit electrified wire along all ledges and protrusions. Both these courses of action must, again, be rejected on the grounds of inhumanity.

Is there nothing I can do to help?

- Surprisingly, yes! Rather obviously, give the horse the management and lifestyle he needs, usually the three Fs: Freedom, Forage and Friends, not to mention grass which always has a soporific effect on horses.
- I have had success in helping calm, relax and reassure horses with 'vices', and helping them reduce the frequency of their performance, by using shiatsu, herbalism, homoeopathy, aromatherapy (*illustrated top right*) and flower remedies (*illustrated right*).
- I have also heard of success by using the Tellington Touch, acupuncture and acupressure (related to shiatsu), clinical nutrition, and the use of nutraceuticals (substances mid-way between feeds and medicines).

27

16 Dealing with a weaver

Weaving is another problem behaviour that seems to be caused mainly by frustration, agitation and anxiety. Unlike crib-biting, wind-sucking and box-walking, however, most weavers only perform this stereotypie when they are emotionally upset. It seems to be similar to the pacing of zoo animals and the body-rocking of disturbed humans.

What is weaving, exactly?

The horse usually stands with his head over his stable door and swings it rhythmically from side to side, often with a deliberate dip as the end of each swing is reached. Often, the horse swings so much that the forefoot on the side away from the direction of the swing leaves the floor – for example, if the head is swinging right, the left forefoot may leave the ground.

Traditionally, people have thought that this puts excess strain on the forelegs although there seems to be no scientific data to support this. Horses tend to weave when over-excited, in anticipation, frustration, anxiety and agitation. It is quite common for a weaver to do so whilst awaiting his feed – he knows it is coming, but he cannot do anything to hurry it up.

The commonly used weaving grilles *do not* stop this behaviour, but frustrate the horse even more: he will probably just weave inside his box, anyway. Tying him up is not the answer, either! It is also unkind and pointless to hang bricks on either side of the doorspace so that he hits his head when he weaves: this is an old, barbaric practice.

How can I help?

- Try to avoid the causative situations: for instance, feed weavers first, not last 'to teach them a lesson' (it doesn't, and can't).
- Keep the atmosphere in the yard very quiet and calm as most weavers dislike activity.
- Never tease the horse in any way, such as by leaving his feed, grooming kit or tack outside his door, but doing nothing about it.
- Make sure he is stabled next to a friend and ideally can touch, smell and mutual-groom with him.
- Do not play a radio in the stable yard: if you use music at all, check first by watching the horse that he is calmed by your choice, not worked up.
- Herbal calmers in the feed can help weaving (and other stereotypies). Also, use as few concentrates as possible, supply ample and varied forage rations, and make sure that you have only sensitive people caring for the horse.
- Complementary/alternative therapies can help 'hyper' horses such as weavers.
- As with other similar problems, weaving is not 'catching'.

17 Dealing with a box-walker

This is another stereotypie that horses seem to perform most of the time. They may tramp, seemingly in a trance, round and round their box, and take little notice of anyone nearby, or even of other horses. It is distressing to watch and can accelerate to the point where the horse works himself into a sweat.

What is the cause of it?

Rather like weaving, this seems to be a behaviour caused initially by anxiety, frustration, worry and similar situations. After a while, usually months, it becomes a confirmed habit and, unfortunately, seems to be impossible to stop; but it can be reduced.

The old remedy was to place straw bales around his path in his box to disturb his movement, but although this may slow a horse down, it seems to frustrate him even more, and certainly does not stop the behaviour.

Tying up the horse ostensibly to get him to rest really frustrates him, and the walking is even worse when he is released.

How can I help?

- Rather like weaving, keep everything as calm and quiet as possible and try to place very placid neighbours next door on both sides of a box-walker. Some are helped by being able to contact their neighbours, but others take no notice of them whatsoever.
- This type of problem, once established, is definitely in the category of what I call 'mind-damage', and is so sad to see.
- Try to calm the horse by means of a quiet yard, few or no concentrates, a low-energy diet if feasible for the horse's work, herbal calmers, homoeopathy, aromatherapy, shiatsu, Tellington Touch and flower remedies. All these things can help.

- His stable needs to be large and have two or more outlooks, with constant fibre and water.
- Study the horse to see if certain circumstances exacerbate the behaviour, and try to reduce or avoid them. For instance, does wearing a rug make the horse worse, the presence or absence of a particular horse or person, the weather, other horses coming and going, dogs in the yard, a stable companion (careful here, for the safety of the other animal), different amounts of turnout, different amounts of exercise and so on?

Unfortunately, this is usually one of those behaviours you just have to live with, but may be able to reduce.

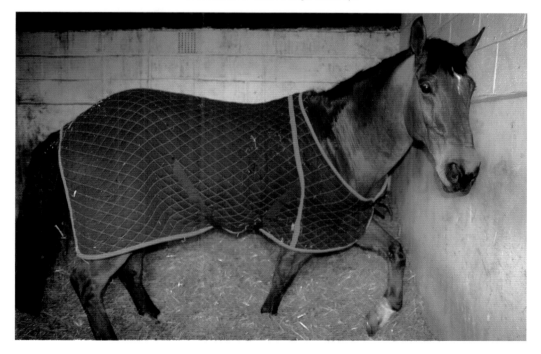

18 Stop your horse eating his bed excessively

Behavioural scientists are now telling us that behaviour problems and stereotypies are less common among horses bedded on straw. Horses are by nature foragers – they enjoy searching for their food. Investigating and rooting in their (straw) beds can be regarded as normal behaviour – but excessive eating of straw can be harmful.

Why do horses eat straw when other forages are available?

The reason for this is that, in nature, horses have a very varied diet to pick and choose from. One scientist found that in one hectare (about two acres) of natural plains grassland there were over 150 different species of grass, herbs and other plants compared with, at most, 16 in a well tended and variably sown domestic field, and often down to as few as six species, almost entirely grasses, in the 'green desert' type of domestic paddock.

A stabled horse only has access to the food/forage he is supplied with. If he is bedded on straw it will almost always be wheat straw, which is high in woody, indigestible fibre (lignin); this is useful, however, for physically breaking up other food passing through the digestive tract, and also for stimulating the wave-like, pulsing movements of the tract (called peristalsis) that push the food along. To the horse, wheat straw is still food of sorts and he will nibble at it, which is fine; but if he is bored with his other forage sources, or does not have enough, he may eat a good deal.

Other forages (fibre such as grass, hay, haylage and branded forages) also contain some lignin. Most meadow-type hay fed to horses can contain about half-a-dozen or more species of grass, but some specialist

hays may contain only one or two. This is obviously highly unnatural, and it is, therefore, quite understandable for the horse to feel a real need to vary his diet however he can.

Horses will also eat their beds if the fibre portion of the diet is insufficient to satisfy (a) their hunger and need to feel full, and (b) their inborn need to chew for a good two-thirds of their time. Remember, too, that it is natural for horses to eat mainly from ground level. Your horse may well prefer, therefore, to eat his bed at ground level than to eat from a less comfortable source such as a net or rack that is positioned as high as his head.

What can I do about it?

- Don't worry about doing too much about it if the horse is not eating large amounts of straw. You could, perhaps, change his bedding to oat straw and/or barley straw if the bed-eating has become a habit, as these are regarded as more suitable for forage than bedding. Changing the horse to an inedible bedding is not the answer, as he obviously needs the roughage and bulk he is getting from the straw, not to mention the entertainment of rooting in it. Have you ever noticed that horses do not root in a shavings bed?

- Make sure that he does have enough fibre and is not actually hungry. Many nutritionists now advise that the fibre portion of the diet of even hard-working horses should not be less than two-thirds of the total ration, measured by weight. There is increasingly a feeling that cereal concentrates (and processed feeds derived from them) should be reduced, or cut out of the diet altogether, except possibly in a few cases of horses in strenuous work; instead the horse should be given high-nutrient forage such as alfalfa, maybe with soaked sugar-beet pulp and oil.

- Give your horse so much fibre that he constantly has some left, *particularly* overnight, when most horses have run out by midnight; unless the horse is really greedy, he will not eat more than he needs. Once you have found out, by trial and error, how much hay or haylage he seems to need over a 24-hour period, you may find that you were not giving him enough – and the straw-eating is almost guaranteed to have decreased a good deal.

- Two things you can do as well are (1) feed your horse's fibre from the ground or from a low level in tubs or special hay holders or mangers; and (2) provide variety by supplying different brands and types of short-chopped forages in large tubs (on the floor, of course) so that he is eating in a more natural and therefore more satisfying way. This makes for increased comfort and contentment and better digestion – an all-round improvement.

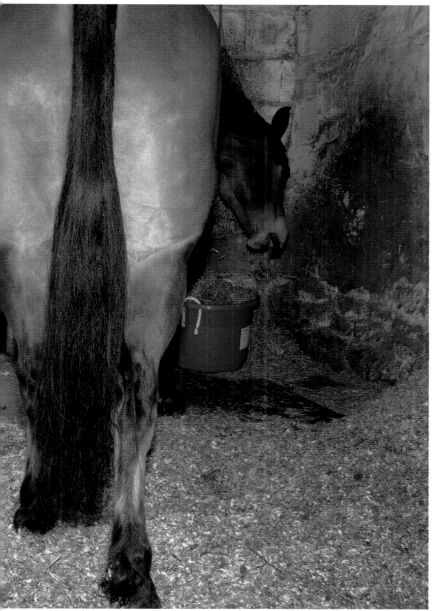

19 Keep a routine to avoid stress

We are usually told (and I have done it myself) to order our stable management into a routine so that horses always know where they stand. It is said that this will promote mental security and confidence in their environment – but is it really as important as we think, and how upsetting is it, if at all, when that routine has to be broken?

Do horses and ponies naturally have a routine?

Observations show that feral horses and ponies are most active at dawn and dusk, often eating more then, interacting with each other and so on. Their main resting and sleeping times are during the night and, to a lesser extent, during the day. Of course, they only actually sleep deeply lying flat out for a very few hours out of 24: studies vary, but they probably sleep this way in 'full recumbency' for about two hours a day, and not all at once. 'Sternal recumbency' (propped on the breastbone) is adopted for lighter sleep, probably another two or three hours, and horses can doze heavily but not actually sleep, apparently, standing up, which is contrary to usual belief.

Stabled horses live in many, very varied environments. Think of the non-stop activities in most riding centres, the afternoon break in racing stables, the often erratic routine in DIY livery yards, the varied shifts of police horses, and so on. Then, of course, there are always special events that completely disrupt a horse's daily home life, such as showing, competitions, hunting, the owner's weekend plans, maybe trips to the farrier. Horses certainly come to know when something usual but out of the daily routine is happening. They may become excited or accept it all – but a break in routine it certainly is.

My experience is that most horses need not be kept on a strictly timed routine, provided that they always have food, water and company available. In time, horses and caring, conscientious owners come to know and trust each other very well, and the horse knows that his needs will be met. Horses with less caring owners are not so fortunate and do, I find, show signs of anxiety and insecurity if things are not done at a certain time – and horses certainly know the time. (This is a little strange when you think that, say, 4pm occurs at differing levels of daylight throughout the year; but the horses still know what time it is!)

With conventional stabling, certainly, the horse is a complete prisoner and has little or no facility to order his own life – if he has been left for so long that he has run out of hay and water, he has no choice but to wait until someone comes and sees to him. He cannot go and graze, drink or socialize, or even exercise when he wants to.

I have a friend who often keeps unusual and erratic hours. Her husband is self-employed and works erratic hours, too, so their evening meal can occur at any time from 7pm to around 10pm. Their two ponies (one working, one retired) are well used to having their supper after that and, if my friend is wide awake during the night, they will often be given some sort of food then, too. They take it in their stride, knowing that food and water are plentifully available, and their owners or a friend will see to their needs during the day as they potter about an old orchard, the stable yard and their open stables.

Conversely, I know of several yards – mainly DIY livery yards, where there is no human manager and no yard routine – where some horses have a set and steady routine, and others do not: the latter show distinct signs of agitation as others are fed, and distress as they are left for hours without fibre and water. (Sadly, other owners' offers of help are often taken as unwanted interference.)

What should I do?

- The main ways to ensure your horse's contentment, routine or no routine, are to see that he *always* has enough hay, haylage or other fibre source and, most vitally, *clean* water.
- Make sure he knows that other horses are nearby, even if he cannot actually be with them – although the latter is ideal. An established routine is fine, as are a few friends to step in when you cannot attend; but don't worry too much if sometimes things go a bit haywire.
- Horses certainly sense discontent or distress in others. Keep your ear to the ground about alternative accommodation for your horse if the lack of organization and reasonable care routine is affecting him.

20 Make sure your horse is not too hot or cold

There is something about buying rugs and clothing accessories that makes owners feel they are doing the right thing by their horses. In reality, few people think accurately about their horse's needs, and many horses are over-rugged/blanketed. Some, though, are clearly cold in their stables. Discomfort creates health and behavioural problems, so how can we tell what a horse needs?

Horses' reactions to temperature

Like other animals, horses vary in their response to changing temperatures. Some curl up at the first sign of a breeze or rain, whilst others actually prefer to be out in the most appalling winter weather, but cannot bear summer with its heat and flies.

In general, horses seem to feel the cold much less than humans. As vegetarians, their natural diet provides 'inner central heating', as long as they have enough of it. Fibrous matter is their natural food: for instance grass (growing or dried) and other plant forages such as herbs, lucerne/alfalfa and clover, as well as the hay, haylage and short-chopped, branded forages so readily available now that we give

stabled domestic horses – and these are mainly carbohydrate foods that provide energy (for work and warmth) in a slow-release, long-term way, largely from cellulose in the cell walls of these plants. It is digested in the horse's large intestine, at the far end of the tract.

The horse's system is adapted to digesting mainly this type of food, and although carbohydrates from cereal grains (starch rather than cellulose) certainly provide concentrated food for energy and warmth, this type of energy comes in short bursts which are soon over, leaving the horse cold and hungry again. Starches and sugars (that are found in growing grass) are digested mainly in the small intestine nearer the start of the tract.

Many horses do strongly dislike

wind and prolonged rain, and these conditions can really chill them. Cold, still, dry weather is quite well tolerated, but a draughty (as opposed to well ventilated), cold stable, a breezy, cold day and a wet coat can lead to severe chilling, even hypothermia.

Conversely, heat stroke is not unknown in horses, and this can be caused by exposure to strong sun (for instance, in fields without a shelter), high humidity on a hot day, or overloading horses with rugs when they are stabled in warm weather. Horses lose heat by sweating: as the moisture evaporates it takes with it excess body heat to cool the body down. This evaporation may not be possible on a humid day, or if the horse is over-rugged.

insulating warm-air layer next to his skin.

- A practical way to check if the horse is hot or cold is simply to feel him. Use the flat of your hand and hold the base of his ears, feel his neck, sides and belly, loins, quarters and flanks. Give time for any heat to pass through the coat to your hand, then use your judgement to see if he feels chilly, too hot, or just right.

Seasonal sense

Remember that just because it is summer it is not necessarily warm, nor is it always particularly cold in winter. Tricky times are often spring and autumn. Don't assume too much. Use the visual and touch tests to be sure. If you are leaving your horse, say, on a spring evening and it seems warm but is likely to turn cold during the night, put a light rug on him. Remember also that unclipped horses often don't need rugging, unless truly very sensitive, except in very cold weather. Leave plenty of fibrous forage to maintain natural heating.

How can I tell if my horse is hot, cold or just right?

- You can tell a lot by just looking at him. It is part of an owner's responsibility to study their horse, because the horse cannot ask for a rug, or a shelter, or to be relieved of clothing.
- If the horse looks tense or anxious, usually shown by tight skin on the face, ears loosely back (rather than sideways as when relaxing), nostrils narrowed and maybe wrinkled up and back, and a worried, depressed or sunken look to the eyes, there is something wrong.
- If the horse is either sweating or shivering, the answer is obvious. Over-heated horses sweat under their rugs particularly, but I have seen horses that have been rugged up, sometimes with two or more rugs, on warm or even hot days, and the sweat has been running down their faces and dripping off their bellies.

- A cold horse will look 'pinched up', and his hair, even if clipped, will appear dull, rough and 'standing on end': it will be standing up away from his body, trying to create an

21 Teach your horse to stale on command

This may seem a strange topic to include in a book on improving a horse's behaviour, but getting your horse to urinate on command, either on to a soft surface or into a bucket, can be very useful. You could practise doing this before and during a long ride or journey, it can help in keeping the bedding drier, and is useful when urine samples are needed.

What are a horse's staling habits?

Both male and female horses and ponies hate staling on to a hard surface (including most types of rubber or synthetic matting) because the urine will splash back on to their legs and bellies. Many people force them to do this by not providing bedding during the day or, sometimes, even at night – to my mind an unacceptable management practice. Under natural conditions, horses would be on grassland or a soft dirt surface so the urine sinks in at once. Although horses may not make nests and beds, they naturally prefer a comfortable surface to lie on. If forced to lie down without bedding, they must lie in their own urine, which can encourage skin problems, and is not good care practice.

How do I teach him?

Watch until the horse is obviously about to stale, and as soon as he starts, give a particular low whistle and praise him. Don't touch him as it might put him off, be quiet and calm, and don't hurry him or stop him in any way; soon he will associate your whistle with staling, and will start to do so 'on command'.

Horses often stale when they come home from a ride and when new bedding is put in their stable, so watch for these times to teach the horse. To get him to stale in a bucket, put a good deal of bedding in the bottom of it so that it does not splash up and put him off, and hold it under the stream of urine. Eventually, when you whistle and hold out the bucket, he will almost surely try to stale.

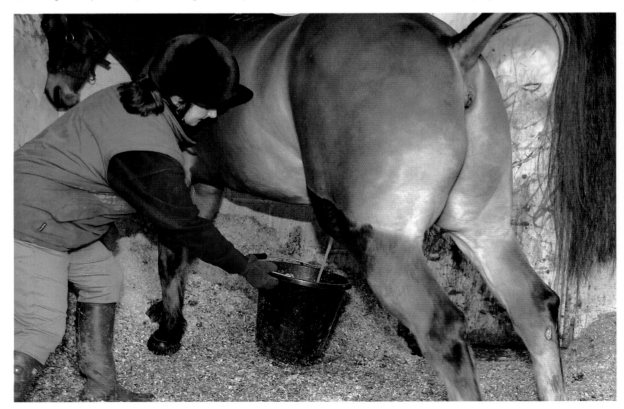

22 Do not keep moving stables

On some yards, horses are moved regularly from one stable to another, sometimes even on a daily basis if accommodation is scarce. Some people seem to do this as a matter of course, and think nothing of it. However, although horses are said not to be territorial in the way that some species of animal are, I am certain that they are to a degree.

What's wrong with moving horses around?

If a horse feels secure in his home and his life, he should regard time in his stable (although not too much of it!) as welcome, where he can, it is hoped, find peace and quiet, plenty to eat and drink, and somewhere dry and soft to lie down – that is, the peace and security of his own place. There is no doubt that a horse knows which is its own box.

It is noticeable that, in those yards where horses are frequently moved around for no good reason except that it suits their attendants, the horses are more on edge, not so 'well behaved', more tense, insecure and anxious. This is definitely not good horse care!

The first thing a horse will do in a new box or home is have a good sniff round. He will be able to smell a previous occupant, unless the box has been properly cleaned out, and this can increase any feeling of insecurity he might already be experiencing. So this is no way to introduce a horse to a new home!

Swapping and changing boxes in a yard where the horse has lived for some time is equally unsettling. Sometimes it may be necessary to change horses around until it is discovered where they are happiest – some like a busy atmosphere, while others need quiet. If a horse is well settled in a box he likes, and another horse is later placed next to him whom he doesn't get on with, it is the newcomer who must be moved. This can be a difficult situation on a livery yard with changing residents, but the horses' contentment is of paramount importance.

How can I help?

Try to have put into a livery contract that the horse's stable will not be changed without your consent, and if it is, make a fuss – politely but firmly – agreement or no. On your own place, allow your horse to live and stay where he is obviously happiest.

23 Playing radios in the stable yard

It is widely believed that horses like music or human voices for company, but I am sure that this is not so. If I go to a yard that is new to me and I hear a radio, I immediately look at the horses nearby, and always notice several who show obvious signs of distress – they are tolerating the noise helplessly.

(not dull) demeanour, alert but relaxed interest, a full, bright eye, and ears flicking unconcernedly towards you. Distress is shown by a tense, even angry expression on the horse's face, and maybe evidence of a stereotypie – head-tossing, grinding the teeth, restlessness – or, conversely, dullness.

Studies on the effects of music on horses have found that quiet, soothing music may actually be welcome, but *in short doses and not when horses are resting*. The type of music that creates tension and stress in stabled horses is anything loud or raucous, disco music, heavy rock and dirge-type music! The sound of constant human voices upsets many horses, too.

What can I do?

- In your own yard, do not leave the radio on for long whether you are there or not.
- Be careful which programmes you choose.
- If inspecting a yard for potential livery facilities, check for radios playing and ask about them: then think carefully about taking your horse there.
- In existing livery, complain if a radio frequently upsets your horse, or you – and leave if the situation does not improve fairly promptly.

Surely a radio playing is better than silence?

Those who spend 'real' time observing horses in either a domestic or a feral environment will first and foremost notice the quietness. It is an utterly relaxing and 'grounding' experience to spend time with horses like this, and to notice how little they use their own voices, and how little constant noise there is in nature.

Although we can rarely achieve this level of silence in domesticity, we can try. The problem with radios is that they never stop unless someone turns them off, and the horses, of course, cannot do this. If you cultivate a perceptive eye for horses' emotions, you will spot at once those who are suffering mental distress because of the radio, those who don't like it very much, and then those happy few who really don't seem to mind it at all.

Calmness is indicated by a quiet

24 Make quietness a golden rule

When I was a child, I was taught unmistakably and for ever to keep quiet around horses. I was running around a stable yard with others, laughing and screaming, when the owner, a big man with a voice to match, stalked up to us, squatted down and whispered: 'Be quiet or go home. Horses *hate* noise and I hate *noisy* children.'

Keeping the noise down

We have mentioned the quietness typical of the natural surroundings in which feral horses and ponies live, and the nervous behaviour a horse might resort to, were he bothered by unwanted noise, such as a radio thoughtlessly left playing all day long.

In the 1980s I was fortunate enough that my work enabled me to follow the horses trained by the late Gordon W. Richards in Cumbria. He was one of the most talented and successful trainers of steeplechasers ever in business, and at that time I was doing a year-long series about his yard for my then magazine *Equi*.

I learned a huge amount of invaluable knowledge and horse-lore during that time, one of which was that the afternoon rest period was sacrosanct. Racing staff start early, but finish at lunch-time, when they are free until tea-time – except on a race day, of course. Once lunch-time arrived, and all the horses had been worked, schooled, grazed in hand and put away or turned out (yes, even horses

in training were turned out), everyone was dismissed from the stable yard.

I never heard anyone shout loudly on that yard – and it was a big establishment – never heard a radio playing, or anyone shout at a horse, or saw anyone run down the yard. No one clattered buckets or shovels unreasonably, but went about their business normally and fairly quietly. The tack room was the exception: here there was a great deal of loud laughter, ribaldry, joking, complaining, teasing and 'unprintables' – but not on the yard.

But my horse isn't a racehorse!

That doesn't matter: the moral here is that, of course, all horses can be treated normally. Most of them have to cope with life and all it brings – with excitement, discipline, work – but there must be no unnecessary noise, and a good deal of 'Quiet Time' firmly slotted into their schedules. No horse or pony is an exception, whatever its breed or job.

The great outdoors

Grass, glorious grass!

The time that your horse spends in the field is, of course, the time when you are least able to control or improve his behaviour. It would almost certainly be very risky to push your way amongst a group of horses when they are playing about with each other (which is undeniably and naturally rough) or worse, having a disagreement, and only a highly confident and competent horseperson with a great deal of experience and intuitive knowledge should do so. Similarly, you cannot stand by your horse all day in order to prevent him being bullied, or bullying others, or 'misbehaving'. So is there anything useful to say about improving your horse's behaviour when he's out?

I think so, because how you organize horses into their different turnout groups – who goes out with who – how you organize paddock layout, as well as when exactly you bring a horse in from the field, or let him out, and the manner in which you do it, can all make a big difference.

It is unfortunate that more and more people with no equestrian background, and little or no quality equestrian education, are nowadays buying horses, and many of them even opening livery yards. As a result, quite a few inappropriate and strange attitudes and policies concerning horse care and management are taking a firm hold in the horse world, to the detriment of the horses they are meant to be benefiting. Accessibility to grazing and decent turnout, even liberty of any kind, is an area where human attitudes have changed very much for the worse, and this is resulting in physically and psychologically deprived horses with resultant behaviour problems. In my professional capacity I am nowadays consulted regularly about such horses.

It is widely known that horses are creatures native to the open grassland plains and prairies. Widely known it may be: acted upon it often is not. Certainly there are some horses who for generations, even thousands of years since their domestication, have been kept stabled for work purposes with little or no turnout; but these were horses who were usually out of their stables for several hours a day in the course of their work, and were often tired when they returned to them. Even so, it is a far from ideal way to keep an animal such as a horse, even though some teaching and other organizations would have us believe differently.

Horses need to graze, and this is an absolutely vital parameter of their existence: they have an inborn, psychological need to chew more or less constantly – they can't help it, it's just the way they are. Anyone looking at horses 'live' in a feral herd, or at domestic ones on decent grazing, can see clearly that this is what they evolved to do – walk about slowly, heads down and swinging from side to side, eating grass for about two-thirds of their 24 hours.

Behavioural problems that have their origins in turnout arrangements, in the quality of freedom on offer (on grass or otherwise), and amongst equine groups, can be resolved to a certain degree with common horse sense. I hope this section helps in this regard.

25 Introduce new horses to a group sympathetically

The way a horse is introduced to new herd mates can have a lasting effect on how well he is accepted by them, and therefore on his future happiness. And if it is done unsympathetically, it may result in his actually being denied acceptance by the group. It can also result in serious injury and psychological distress, or in a disrupted and unstable group.

No guarantee of a failsafe way

We know that feral horses live in mainly family groups in the wild. Some experts believe that the stallion is 'the boss', others that there is a 'lead mare' and that the stallion is the protector and progenitor, not the leader. Also, some believe that there is actually no 'kicking order' or herd hierarchy, whilst others, just as well qualified and experienced, state categorically that there is a hierarchy or rank order, particularly between youngsters and their elders, but also between individuals regardless of sex or age.

All this can be quite perplexing to horse owners who simply want their horse to have friends and be turned out with them in relative safety. There is no doubt that introducing a new horse to an established group, kicking order or not, can be fraught with risk if it is not done thoughtfully and carefully. Also, introducing a new horse on, say, a livery yard to others who may comprise a changing or unstable group (that is, they are not necessarily always all turned out together due to owners' requirements, horses being lame, and so on) can also cause trouble.

Even with those horses who know each other well and are regularly turned out together, there is no guarantee of absolute safety. The modern practices of either not turning them out at all (which is unacceptable in my view)

or turning them out into very small, individual paddocks (better than nothing, I suppose) do not give horses their essential experience of something approaching normal social interaction. Accepting that there is some risk (which is greatly lessened if the horses are not shod), let's look at wrong and then right ways to introduce a horse to others.

The wrong way

Simply take your horse to the field, bundle him in with the others, and let him take pot luck. If he is a domineering, confident type he will probably get at least one of them before they get him. If he is more reticent or laid back, he will probably be roughly investigated and may suffer front end/foreleg injuries due to foreleg strikes from at least one of the others, and then one of the group may lay into him. He could be seriously injured, or if he is lucky, ostracized, so that he must take up station either at the very edge of the group or well away from it. Neither will make him happy, and the whole episode will at least temporarily upset the others.

A better way

As an initial safety precaution, it is infinitely preferable that the horses are not shod, ideally neither in front nor behind. In any case, feet and shoes must be in good order, with no sharp edges or raised clenches as these could cause cuts, and no studs or raised nail-heads/road nails, which could intensify the force of an impact. Protective, high-impact boots can protect the lower legs from kicks, and over-reach boots on all four feet can protect against treads, self-inflicted or otherwise, during any scrambles to get out of each other's way. Rugs may protect against body blows, though they can also get caught in flying hooves.

- Remove all headcollars/halters.
- Turning horses out hungry should distract them from politics and encourage them to graze.
- Pick from the group the friendliest, most laid-back horse or pony and lead him in hand with yours. Let them sniff and touch each other whilst held. I prefer to use double-length lead ropes or half-length lunge reins so you can stay out of the way but still have control.
- Hack them together and maybe stable them next to each other.
- Then turn them into a paddock, just the two of them, for a day or so.
- Next, take the next most friendly horse from the group and introduce him or her in the same way; ...
- ...and so on until your horse has met all the group members, and is spending time in the original, familiar paddock with the gradually increasing group until they are all together and integrated.
- Horses feel safest in large fields, so choose the largest one you can in the early days so that during the settling-in period there are plenty of escape routes.

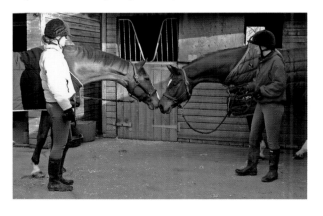

26 Protect your horse against bullying

They say that bullying is normally a horse's way of trying to inch his way up the herd hierarchy. Although he may never succeed (see page 52, Understand the herd hierarchy), there is no doubt that bullying causes unrest, loss of condition and possible injury. Some say that nature should be left to sort things out, but in my experience this rarely happens. What to do?

Banish the bully, not the bullied

Bullies are as unwelcome among a herd of horses as they are in a school playground. Human bullies are normally either cowards who pick on those weaker than themselves, immature people put in positions of power, or fairly tough but insecure people seeking to establish superiority, or just those who like picking fights – provided they are not going to get beaten; and these categories apply to horses, too.

There is a general feeling that horses on the receiving end of bullying should be removed from the herd and grazed with a quiet, non-threatening companion. However, a more

effective way of dealing with the issue is to remove the bully, because if he isn't bullying your horse, he'll probably bully someone else's. Furthermore, removing the bully should not disturb the herd's established social structure, because most horses like a quiet life and generally with the bully removed, peace will reign.

In a public yard such as a livery yard, a reasonably businesslike and conscientious proprietor will appreciate the problem and perhaps fence off a smaller paddock for the bully, with maybe a horse who is tougher than he and will not stand for being bullied. Friendships do have to be considered, though, and if the bully has to be alone but in sight of other horses (maybe with animals of another

species such as cattle or sheep), then this may have to be so, for the sake of safety and calm.

There are undoubtedly bullies in feral herds too, but although the horses may wish to remain in a fairly close group, there is room for any harassed member to gallop away from the bully without his route being blocked or diverted by fences. In domesticity, horses may well not have the room to escape a bully as they would in the wild, so it is unlikely that they will 'sort themselves out' without injury.

Even if a horse superior to the bully is introduced, the bully normally keeps away from him and picks on others. The superior horse, too, will not normally protect other horses. Horses usually only protect close friends, relatives and maybe owners with whom they have special relationships.

Nor is the bully going to be stopped by your remaining in the field and trying to punish him for attacking your horse. This situation could quickly escalate into a dangerous, high-speed free-for-all.

Preferential treatment may help

There was a very interesting opinion expressed many years ago in *Equine Behaviour*, the members' journal of The Equine Behaviour Forum (see Useful Addresses page 150), about an effective way of raising a horse's status or image in a herd. This involves paying the horse a lot of positive, desirable attention in front of other horses – fussing him, praising him, stroking, grooming, leading him out to do interesting things where others can see, grazing him in hand whilst they are stabled, riding in a non-forceful way and praising him publicly for just being gorgeous.

Conversely the horse must never be either corrected, punished or stressed in front of any of the other horses, and the handlers must never actually fuss other horses in his presence, simply work with them normally. He should be first in the group to be fed, first to be led to the field or stables, and physically kept in superb condition by correct feeding and physical fitness. This last aspect makes the horse feel really well in himself and this always helps with self-confidence. (Do not, though, feed the horse where others can get at him as this could be dangerous.) In short, the horse is seen by the others to be a special individual.

I always remembered this, and tried it with my first horse when he had to move to a new, well-established group in a yard where I was not allowed to make 'correct' introductions and where the horses chased him away. It took a few weeks but it worked very well, and once he was 'elevated' in the eyes of the other horses, he kept his superior position. I recommend it as well worth a try. (I should add that some people with a scientific background believe that this will not work because horses are not interested in status.)

27 Let your horse know it's all right to be caught

A horse that won't be caught probably causes us as much frustration as one with any other equine 'failing'. If only we could outrun him, there would be no problem. It's so infuriating! It's surely not much to ask him to come in so his owner, who pays his bills after all, can go for a little ride? Unfortunately the horse doesn't see it that way.

Why won't he come to me? I never hurt him

First of all, don't take offence. It could be nothing that you have done to your horse which makes him this way, but something someone else has done to him in the past – unless, of course, he has started this trick since you bought him. If he associates coming in with something unpleasant, such as work that may be uncomfortable, stressful, difficult or actually painful, or being shut in a boring stable for too long, he can't be blamed for not obliging you.

Your plan of action must be to make him want to come in, or at least not to mind it – and that means enjoyment.

How to do it

- Try taking a large, white, rustly bag of mints and other titbits into the field and walking around near him but ignoring him and letting him see you eat the sweets yourself: this often works very well. It is best to use this technique when your horse is out with only one other quiet friend (especially if you feed it), otherwise you could be overrun by a mint-seeking mob.
- Always turn him out in a field-safe headcollar with a catching strap on it.
- Start this retraining by getting the horse to come to you in a small yard or boring manège, rewarding and praising him, leading him around, maybe giving him a small feed, and then letting him go out again.
- Sometimes just catch the horse and stand with him for a few minutes, then lead him in (or let him go) so that he does not immediately associate being caught with being taken away.

Once your horse associates being caught with nothing awful and maybe something nice, you can dispense with titbits (which can cause trouble in a group).

28 Catch your horse safely in a group

This can be quite tricky, and much depends on the attitude of the other horses, not only your own. A group containing a horse that attacks people, whether coming to get him or not, is always dangerous, as is any group that charges round an approaching human, even in a friendly way. You may need the co-operation of other owners …

Group tactics

You would think that horses would be glad to stay in the field, but no – if one is going out, they often all want to go out, particularly if either the grazing or the weather – or both – is not very appealing.

Most horses will actually keep back if you command or shout 'back' and push them away. If the group is neither too aggressive nor too big, a water pistol set on a strong jet is quite a good weapon. If a horse comes too close and won't stay back, you subtly give him a strong squirt on his muzzle and command 'back' at the same time. This works quite well for biters and nippers, too.

If the situation really gets out of hand, you will need help to ward off other horses whilst you get yours out

– everyone staying calm and assertive at the same time. Your helper/s can have water pistols and lead ropes (ideally pale coloured, as these are more easily seen), and whirl them in the face of any oncoming horses: this usually keeps them back.

Consider a retraining programme for all the horses in the group, because horses that mill around are actually badly trained and ill-mannered. Start by making it a rule never to take food into such a group. Then catch up the horses individually, lead them around the field, and then let them go. Eventually remove single horses and either keep them out, or return them. Keep calm and strong, and insist on discipline from people and horses. The horses will get used to people coming and going, and to being caught and let go, and the problem usually subsides.

29 Teach your horse to leave the others

Horses that won't leave the others in a field are as bad as those that won't be caught at all. You've caught your horse, but on the way to the gate he naps, plants, jibs and may start trying to circle, sit down, rear up – anything but leave his friends and go with you. Why does he do it, and what can you do about it?

Why the problem starts

This is a clear case of the horse preferring to be with his friends than with his owner. The two have clearly not 'bonded', and the horse does not regard his owner as his other half, or as someone to be respected and good to be with. In short, he actually feels safer with the herd than with his person. Another possibility is that he has not yet had enough grass and just does not want to come in.

What can I do?

- If a horse naps under these circumstances, he will often start to go forwards again if you first turn him smartly in a few small circles, then aim for the gate again, commanding 'walk on' – and if he persists in being nappy, then you will have to do more circles, or back him towards the gate if necessary, and thus gradually proceed. Every time he makes one step towards the gate, praise him instantly.
- You could give him a mint as long as none of the other horses notices you doing so – otherwise don't do it, because it could be dangerous.
- If you're still having trouble, try to turn him out in a very small, boring enclosure with one other horse and practise catching him up and bringing him out. He is almost certain to come with you. Get him very used to his name and the command 'walk on', maybe on the lunge or during in-hand lessons, and praise him instantly when he co-operates.
- As he improves, try him in the larger field again, and then, as a matter of course, be more assertive, safe and fun to be with. Horses either dislike or disregard people whom they consider to be weak, and some will positively take advantage of them.
- If you behave more confidently – being calm, firm and positive – and improve your relationship with your horse, the problem will almost certainly go away.

30 Teach your horse to be patient while you open a gate

It could be a potentially dangerous situation if your horse is hopping and jigging around whilst you are trying to negotiate a gate, particularly one on to a public road – especially if it is not properly hung so that it drags on the ground, has to be lifted up at the catch end before it will move, and is generally as much trouble as your horse.

First things first

If it is your gate, the first task is really to get it mended so that it hangs properly. A gate should open and close easily so that you can hold it open with one hand while you either lead or ride the horse through the gateway.

- Next, train your horse to obey implicitly the command 'Stand'. I think this is the most important word a horse can learn, because if he is standing still he can't cause any trouble. Simple groundwork in a small enclosure is the way to start. Lead your horse near the fence, and as you reach a corner where he cannot go forward or swing away from you because of the fence, immediately say 'stand'. Praise him instantly if you get even a second or two of stillness. Then turn the horse's head round the corner, and

say 'walk on'. Continue round the school fence to the next corner and repeat the exercise; again, praise the horse if he stands. That's enough for one session.

- Next day, or later that day, ask for a few more seconds, along the fence but not in a corner, and progress like that until you can get him to do it in

the middle of the arena, and to wait till you say 'walk on'.

- The next stage is to be able to walk a few steps away and have him stand still while you do so, then return and praise him.
- If the horse jigs about, say a firm 'no', and calmly keep putting him back where you first asked him to stand, and say 'stand' again until he is thoroughly fed up and obeys. As in all training, you must behave as though you have absolutely no doubt whatsoever that he will co-operate.
- The key to success is persistent insistence, even if minor progress takes all day! Instant praise ('good boy') is essential, and so, I believe, is instant correction ('no'). Titbits are not essential once the horse properly understands 'good boy'.
- Once he will stand, and walk on, on command, opening and shutting gates is no problem.

49

31 Feed your horse safely in the field

Most domestic groups of equines are a mixed bunch, all shapes and sizes, all different breeds or no breed at all, and with completely different dietary needs. Being on the same grass paddock together is no more than a starting point, because their dietary differences will need to be addressed by varied supplementary feeding. Some will not need any at all; others might be seriously short of an essential nutrient. How to cope safely?

What's yours is mine ...

Even if horses are full of grass, gorged, over-indulged and weighed down, if someone comes into the field with a bucket they will all come over to see what other goodies might be had for the taking. Clearly in such a situation you could be at serious risk of being kicked or knocked over, unless there were only a very few, well-behaved animals, and you all knew each other really well.

Even so, in my opinion feeding one horse safely in amongst a field of others is impossible unless there is a fenced-off area where he can be fed on his own. And if this area is in view of the other horses, they will probably squirm around outside trying to get at the favoured horse's feed; and then when he is put back with them, pent-up jealousy, anger and frustrations could be let loose on him – and you might get caught up in the mêlée.

What can I do?

- The only safe way to feed a single horse in a herd of others is to do so out of sight and reach of them. Even so, he will smell of food when he gets back to them, so it will help to graze him in hand after his feed for a few minutes in order to disguise the smell.
- Buckets with each horse's correct rations can be given in the field communally if there are enough humans to ensure control whilst they eat. Catch the most dominant first, plus any bullies, and so on down the line. Let them all go only when the last has finished, and be sure to remove all the buckets.
- Otherwise bring them all in to be fed in their individual stables or in feeding stalls inside their barn in the paddock, then they can be let out again. This latter is common on mainland Europe but not in the UK.

32 Coping with an escape artist

We've probably all met those horses or ponies able to wriggle through apparently any hedge, or jump any fence or gate – and you have to admire them. Is it intelligence, or a stronger-than-average instinct to be free that drives them to escape? It may be a bit of both, but one thing is for sure: it is a risky and potentially expensive trait.

The law and the insurance companies

Certainly in the UK the law considers it is the responsibility of the owner of an animal to control it and make sure that it is kept safely where it is meant to be, where it can do no harm. If it does cause harm and/or damage, even to an unwanted intruder, it is the owner who is liable.

If a straying animal causes damage or injury (eats crops, causes a road accident, kicks or bites another animal or a person), the owner is liable even if he or she had taken all reasonable precautions to prevent it; this is called 'strict liability' and should be covered in all insurance policies. It even applies in cases where horses are let out, unknown to the owner, by mischief makers or vandals.

What can I do?

- All perimeter fences, hedges, walls, doors and gates should be much higher and more secure than most are now, not only to keep horses in, but also to discourage intruders.
- A few horses can jump very high fences and wide dykes and will go walkabout on their own, so company is not the answer. Most don't, even though they could. If you own one of the former, your only chance is to tether him securely and safely within a field on his own, out of reach but within sight of others…
- …or to construct exceptionally high fencing for him.
- Normal escape artists may be kept in by reinforcing hedges with strong fencing on one or both sides (which is expensive), or by putting electric fencing inside the hedge or fence to deter them.
- Don't forget the gates! Horse fencing and gates should be at least the height of the horses' withers, and hedging should be thick and ideally prickly, right down to the ground.

33 Understand the herd hierarchy

At the time of writing, this is one of the most controversial subjects in the field of equine behaviour. Some experts maintain that there is definitely a hierarchy or 'kicking order', whilst others claim that there isn't. Most 'ordinary' horse owners believe that there is – but is this because traditionally we have been told that there is?

How are feral and domestic herds structured?

The answer to this question is, quite differently! Feral herds consist of a stallion and mature females with their youngstock; herds are mainly family groups, although new mares may enter existing herds sometimes. The long-term core of the herd comprises the mares and their offspring. Apart from

breeding, they manage well without the stallion, who is actually a temporary member in the life of the herd, most stallions holding sway for only a few years whilst they are at their physical peak and able to fend off usurpers.

Domestic herds generally consist of a motley mixture of geldings and mares, ponies and horses – except on a stud farm, where the herd structure would be more natural. Only in private ownership, and not always then, is there much stability in the herd structure, as in a livery yard,

owners and their animals come and go frequently – an unnatural state of affairs, as far as the horses are concerned.

Is there a leader, or not?

From many years of experience and observation, I would propose that there is a hierarchy of sorts, but that it is not a clear top-to-bottom one. There is often a wise or self-confident senior mare (not necessarily old) whose

example others may follow, and there may be stallion-like geldings (not necessarily rigs) who try to keep mares for themselves.

From a practical point of view, however, individual friendships regardless of sex are far more important to the horses than status – and so the current fashion of grazing mares and geldings separately is quite senseless: if horses get on well there is no need for this – and it would certainly be foolish to turn out together horses of either sex who do not get on. This will deliberately create a fraught and potentially dangerous situation, particularly as most domestic horses, other than breeding stock, are shod.

In overcrowded conditions horses do appear to become more tense, and to create a kind of hierarchy: and again, overcrowding is relatively common in the modern domestic situation. However, it is my experience that if you turn out friends of both sexes together and give them enough room, there are unlikely to be problems.

53

34 Help a horse who hates rugs

Rugs are obviously a human invention to keep horses warm. They are completely unnatural and some horses show their dislike of them, which may amount to distress, by rubbing themselves, ripping the rugs and doing anything they can think of to get rid of the hated garment. It's an expensive, upsetting habit. Can we help at all?

Reconsider rugs and clipping

Naturally we want our horses to be warm and comfortable, but there's a lot more to this than just clipping a horse so that he does not sweat in work, and then putting a rug of the right size on him. It has to fit his shape and suit his movement as well.

Many horses are clipped who really do not need to be: to my mind there is a strong case against clipping a horse at all, especially if it is more extensively than is strictly necessary, just for appearance's sake. 'Smartness' should never come before equine well-being.

What can I do?

- First ensure that your horse is not too warm under his rugs and that the fabric is permeable ('breathable'). Make sure also that he does not have a skin problem, as this could cause him discomfort. Choose the lightest and softest rug/s you can find (see Useful Addresses: for instance, Goldson Rugs make lovely acrylic fleece rugs), but use them as little as possible. Wash them in non-allergenic laundry products in case the detergent and fabric conditioner are causing the problem.
- Whatever rug you use must be as comfortable as possible. There must be no heavy pressure on any part of the horse (normally the top of the withers, the points of the shoulders and the points of the hips) as this will cause discomfort. The rug must be very roomy around the shoulders and hips so that it does not inhibit the horse's movement.
- Make sure your horse's box is well ventilated, but not damp or draughty, both of which make the air feel colder. The bed, too, must be dry -- most are not.
- If you and your horse are still having problems, consider keeping him without rugs. If he is doing little or no work this should not be a problem provided he has a good shelter in his field; but if he is working fairly actively and sweats up, you can try helping him to maintain a lighter

winter coat so that clipping and rugging can be kept to a minimum.

Maintaining a lighter winter coat

Comfortable, lightweight rugging and sensible feeding help, but the most effective factor is to expose your horse to 16 hours out of 24 of full-spectrum daylight, natural or artificial. The amount of daylight entering the pupils of the horse's eyes signals to his brain what time of year it is and, therefore, what kind of coat he needs to grow.

The more progressive Thoroughbred studs that sell yearlings in the autumn start to gradually maintain the amount of light at 16 hours from the summer solstice (21 June in the northern hemisphere) so that the animals' brains do not detect a lessening in daylight hours and so keep their summer coats. You can continue this regime until the winter solstice (21 December), when the year turns and the days begin to lengthen again; at this time the coat will naturally and gradually begin to be cast, and the new summer coat to grow.

Check the times for sunrise and sunset, and by putting the lights on in your horse's box morning and evening, always ensure that he experiences 16 hours of light a day out of 24, and eight hours of darkness. This will maintain a lighter winter coat.

What kind of light?

The best type of light is the full-spectrum light that is closest to natural daylight: you could use the type of light sold to correct SAD (seasonally affected disorder) in humans, suitable brands being Daystar and Activa. Plant lights used in commercial nurseries will also do. A 150 to 200watt ordinary light bulb works quite well, but not the ordinary blue spectrum fluorescent lights – these can actually make some people and animals feel unwell.

It has been found that one hour's exposure to the light between 2am and 3am has a similar effect to the longer exposure period, but you would need a timer switch to use this method. It would also be kinder to use a fitting that brings the lights on and turns them off gradually.

35 Occupying the horse on restricted grazing

Many horses and ponies experience restricted grazing, partly because of the risk of laminitis, and partly, in the UK at least, due to the shortage of land. However, horses can become bored when grass is sparse and areas small. So how can we help?

Horses' preference?

Undoubtedly, horses prefer tasty grass! This does not necessarily mean short, young grass, contrary to popular opinion: in fact the species of grass is more important, and ryegrasses, traditionally sown for horses, are not the favourites of most of them. A more varied and generous mix of meadow-type grasses keeps them busy and happily grazing. Other plants such as clover and herbs are welcomed, too.

So how can I keep my horse entertained?

- If possible, have your paddock/s sown with a wide mixture of meadow grasses. There are mixes for all categories of horse or pony these days, which will help keep them interested and correctly nourished. Include a separate herb strip and a little clover.
- When the grass is sparse and the area small, you can help by scattering succulents such as horse carrots and bruised or misshapen eating apples (often cheap from shops) on the ground. Some horses also like turnips and other roots. Don't worry about the nutritional value (although be careful with apples) because the sugar content of roots is low – they are about 98 per cent water and fibre.
- Supply hay or haylage in holders or nets around the area. Small-hole nets and holders that ration the amount available in one bite are good. Scatter feeding points in various places to keep the horses on the move.
- Large areas with poor grazing are always better and more interesting for horses than smaller areas with rich grass – and horses like stables and paddocks with a view, and a variety of features such as trees and shrubs, uneven land and shallow ponds, all of which keep them more interested and occupied.
- Some people put toys in their paddock such as footballs, or feeder-balls with low-energy/high-fibre cubes in them.
- Of course, horses are nearly always happier with company, either equine or some other species.

36 Keep things calm when turning out

I know people who will not turn their horses out themselves because they are so hard to handle. I also know horses that used to be calm and well behaved to turn out, but because of poor technique on the part of helpers or staff in the owner's absence, have become dangerously silly and wild. How do you restore calm and a sensible demeanour?

General points to consider

Horses can become silly with people whom they do not respect, and so groundwork exercises to establish some kind of sensible authority are a good idea – voice training, backing in hand (head down), walk on, stand when told (most important), also long-reining and controlled lungeing.

Is there an apparently dominant horse? If so, he or she would normally lead the group, and the others would follow in rank order. Walk out friends together. Ordinary headcollars offer little control, so consider learning to use a controller headcollar or a nose chain (see page 106) for difficult customers, or leading out in a bridle.

How to go about it

At turnout time, give the horses a little food, maybe with pulled grass in it, so they are not so hungry that they cannot wait to get at the grass. Use confident, strong-minded handlers capable of maintaining a calm, firm and positive demeanour. Carrying a whip may help with some horses, to tap the chest for slowing down or the hindquarters to control swinging. Use an unvarying routine that the horses will get to learn quickly, and will respect.

- The leader opens the gate with one hand and takes her horse through;
- as she does so, she passes the gate to the next one, and then…
- …stands the horse up and waits.

- The second person does the same, and so on, so the gate is never left hanging loose.
- The last person fastens it and joins the line. All animals must face the fence.
- At the same time, headcollars are unfastened, but…
- …are held in place for a few seconds whilst the horses are told to stand.
- When everyone is ready, they are

quietly dropped off the horses' necks.
- Finally, to teach the horses to wait, they can all be given one titbit at the same time.
- The handlers step back, and the horses will turn on their hind legs – this way, handlers will be well out of reach of any kicked-up hind hooves.
- Job done.

37 Prevent your horse waiting at the gate all day

There are occasions and circumstances when horses appear not to want to be out. Many owners cannot understand this, and fail to recognize that horses hanging around the gate is a clear signal that they want to come in. A domestic field is not 'the wild' and may not be nearly so appealing – but what can be done about it?

Why do they do this?

To many people it is really perplexing when horses stand around by the field gate, and a habit that many feel powerless to stop. But just as many also appreciate that horses only ask to come in when they are unhappy out -- so it is incumbent upon us to get to the bottom of the issue and find out what the problem is. It can include:

- being afraid of a bully horse;
- a friend having been left in the stables;
- extremes of weather (too hot, too cold, prolonged rain or hail, strong wind, flies);

- lack of food or water;
- no shelter;
- associating the field with a frightening incident.

How can I help?

The only way you can hope to stop your horse doing this and make him happier and more relaxed in his field is to find a solution to the reasons he does it. This may be difficult if you keep your horse in rented accommodation or at livery, but it is the only way, so you may need to speak to whoever is in charge, or to other owners if there is no manager.

First check your field for grazing,

shelter and water. If there is a bully or other enemy, it is that horse who should be removed, not your horse. If your horse's friend cannot be turned out and this is the reason, yours may be happier left with him or her. Decide if the weather conditions really are suitable to turn horses out: most hate extremes of weather and, of course, flies, and will probably be more content indoors with company.

If the horse associates the field with a frightening incident, then this will be difficult to obliterate -- though it may well happen in time. If it doesn't, however, you should really try to find a different field.

Healthy and happy

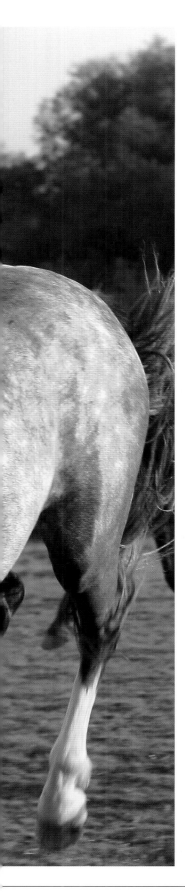

Do horses have emotions?

Nothing affects a horse's behaviour more than the way he is feeling. This also applies to us, and to probably every other living creature, so it is not hard for us to empathize with our horses, or to put ourselves in their place. If you feel sick or are in pain you are not interested in your work; if you are frightened, all your attention is on whatever is causing it, and you don't pay attention to those around you; if your life partner is missing from your life you feel bereaved and devastated, possibly afraid and insecure – but if everything is right with your world, you may feel like jumping for joy.

The problem with empathizing is that it has not been a fashionable thing to do. We have been told constantly by teaching organizations not to anthropomorphize or credit horses with human feelings or emotions. Some very eminent horse people have said and written – and still do, even now – that it is wrong, and shows a lack of understanding to believe that horses experience similar emotions to humans. They cannot rationalize, they say, and do not possess the ability of logic; nor do they experience happiness or sadness – and these people even maintain that because horses cannot solve problems, understand their lives, have 'an agenda', plan ahead or remember much at all, they do not have the faculty of being able to think, and operate in a purely mechanistic way.

These people are clearly wrong, and many not at all eminent horse people know that; moreover, from my contacts over the years with members of the Equine Behaviour Forum and others, some have even been made to feel silly for disagreeing. Others understandably look askance at, or down on, those who believe in that very Victorian concept. If you read pre-Victorian equestrian literature, that arrogant opinion does not come over at all. Anna Sewell's *Black Beauty* began to change that convenient but erroneous view, but it is taking a very long time. Humans are most comfortable with the familiar, and old ideas die hard. Many also find it easy and convenient not to have to think, so they just go along with the status quo.

Some scientific writers do state that horses' emotions and feelings are similar to those of humans and other mammals. From a behavioural aspect, a healthy and *happy* horse is much more rewarding to deal with: he is more outgoing, more willing to relate to us and co-operate with us, and shows far fewer behavioural problems – if, indeed, he shows any at all – than a repressed, oppressed, depressed, ill-used, misunderstood and badly managed one.

38 Feed more forage and fewer concentrates

We have already discussed the premise that horses evolved and are best adapted to eat grass and other vegetation, and that starchy food from cereal grains has never formed a significant part of the wild or feral horse's diet. But we know that Derbys and Badmintons have been won on oats, so concentrates can't be all that bad, can they? Well actually, yes, they can…

Would you please elaborate...

The horse's digestive system is not very efficient, and can be easily upset if given unsuitable food: not only mouldy forage, but also too many concentrates. What constitutes too many? For some horses, that means any at all, and there is a move in the field of nutritional science to feed concentrates only to certain categories of horse: those in strenuous work (racehorses, three-day eventers, two-day-a-week hunters in galloping countries, 100-mile-a-day endurance horses), and older Thoroughbreds or debilitated horses.

It is known that high concentrate/low fibre diets favour the development of gastric ulcers. Saliva is alkaline, and buffers the acid produced by the digestive juices in the system – but the trouble is that saliva is only produced when the horse actually chews, whereas acid is produced all the time. Too much acid can damage the gut lining and cause ulcers. Some starch can arrive down into the large intestine before it has been digested, upsetting its chemical balance and killing off the micro-organisms there which digest fibre, causing colic. All this makes the horse feel ill, in pain and far from happy.

What can I do?

Nowadays we have a good choice of variable energy, high nutrient, short-chopped forage feeds such as dried alfalfa/lucerne, clovers, grasses and feeding straws, and we can supply the correct energy levels for every category of horse, whether resting or in hard work, without the starch found in cereal grains, or feeds made from them, such as coarse mixes (US: sweet feeds) and some horse nuts. This is particularly so if soaked sugar-beet pulp and maybe extra oil are added to the feed.

Also, give the horse generous amounts of hay or haylage so that he never runs out of food. Horses fed this way very rarely gorge, they remain psychologically and physically occupied, and feel well and contented. Very greedy animals may need rationing, however.

39 If your horse is a 'plodder', think why

Riding a horse that 'just won't go' can be quite the opposite of enjoyable. No one likes having to work the whole time to achieve that famous forward movement, particularly if we are clearly not succeeding. Lack of energy is often felt to be a feeding matter, and sometimes it is – but could there be other reasons for apparent sluggishness?

Why does my horse have no energy?

The reasons for a lack of energy might include the following:
- Assuming that the horse is healthy and sound, the most prevalent reason for lack of 'go' is the horse's temperament. No matter what some people may say, there are undoubtedly horses that are just lazy: they can't be bothered to work, and that's that.
- The horse doesn't understand that he is required to move more energetically. This is due to a lack of proper teaching of the aids, and a failure to establish 'the forward ethic' in schooling.
- A rider who gives a leg aid at every stride. He/she does this to create more energy, but because it happens all the time it actually has a dulling effect on the horse and he comes to ignore, and tolerate, it.
- His diet is insufficient in energy for his work. This may apply even though he is not underweight.

What can I do?

- Pick the horse for the job, and if you have a genuinely laid back, non-athletic horse, don't expect him to 'ping' when it comes to energetic work or work he really dislikes

– manège work, for instance, as opposed to hacking out. Forcing him to do something he doesn't like is not productive or kind.
- If lack of understanding is the problem, reschool him to understand the forward aids (upbeat mental attitude from the rider, response to the leg, maybe a *tap* from the whip, vocal encouragement). As soon as you get a response you should immediately *cease the aid*. When he slips back again, repeat until he maintains the pace unbidden. Naturally, don't unreasonably restrict him with the bit or he will become confused, resistant, heavy and unwilling.
- Try a higher energy diet, following the advice of a nutritionist. Often highly concentrated feeds such as oats without husks (starting with a handful in each feed) make a big difference – but sometimes they just pile weight on. If that happens, temperament, training and inclination are the problems, not feeding.

40 Avoid foods that make your horse hard to handle

There is no point in giving yourself 'a double handful' of horse if you don't have to. Over-confinement has a lot to do with excess energy, of course, but feeding can certainly cause it, particularly the traditional view that 'hard work needs hard feed'.

What can I do?

- Simply feed as little cereal-based feed as possible. Always try a horse on an all-fibre diet first, such as ad lib hay or haylage, plus a short-chopped forage feed of a suitable energy grade, from 7 megajoules of digestible energy per kilogram for resting horses, laminitics or good doers, to 12MJ of DE or more for hard-working horses.
- Add succulents such as sugar-beet pulp, carrots, other roots and apples and/or grass, of course.
- Extra oil can add energy for harder work without 'hyping up' the horse, and a broad-spectrum (wide-ranging) vitamin and mineral supplement should ensure his nutrient levels.

This type of feed and feeding regime is better for his digestion, metabolism and his temperament.

Why do hard feeds 'hot' horses up?

Hard feed means concentrates: this is traditionally oats, but nowadays also high-energy cubes and coarse mixes, or any cereal-based feed with an energy content higher than, say, 10 megajoules of digestible energy per kilogram (check the analysis panel on the bag), or at any rate higher than the horse needs. Cereals commonly fed to horses in the western hemisphere and Australasia include oats, barley and maize (corn). Others are fed to horses in other countries, depending on availability.

Cereals provide a quick boost of high energy from starch, which is digested mainly in the small intestine immediately following the stomach. If the amounts are too high to be fully digested before the gut movement pushes the food on to the large intestine, which is meant mainly to digest fibre, starch flows into this part of the gut and can cause a chemical imbalance unfavourable to the resident gut micro-organisms that digest the fibre. These therefore stop working properly or die, decompose, and cause further problems which can lead to colic and laminitis but also excitability, aggressiveness and discomfort – not conducive to calm, controlled energy.

41 Have your saddle checked regularly

Many apparently obscure behaviour problems occur under saddle because of saddles which are not even painful, just slightly uncomfortable in some cases. It's easy to forget that a horse's shape changes throughout the year even if he is in constant work, but the saddle stuffing can change, too, resulting in a troublesome mismatch.

Saddle fit and horse shape

A saddle is meant to make life more comfortable for horse and rider. Some of those stockier animals with a wide back are very comfortable to ride bareback, but sitting on sweat is not particularly pleasant. Other horses, even when in good condition, have a backbone that is easily felt by the rider's seat, even if it doesn't actually protrude; therefore most horses are ridden with a saddle.

From animal skins and textile pads we have progressed to high-tech, scientifically designed saddles with built-in padding or stuffing to cater for all human and equine shapes and disciplines. We all know that neither saddle nor padding (numnah, blanket) should touch the spine anywhere, but they must also not rub (friction) – although some movement is unavoidable – and the pressure they exert must be as even as possible.

If horses (a) put on weight or (b) develop different muscles due to continuing, correct riding, a saddle can become too narrow: this will be felt behind and below the withers in particular, and down behind the shoulder blades. The saddle may sit differently on the back, too, causing

uneven pressure and poor balance, and it may rub the loin area. Uneven muscle development due to an incorrect way of going can cause discomfort, and loss of weight or muscle wastage can also make a significant difference to saddle fit.

The only way that horses can tell us that they are experiencing discomfort or pain from a badly fitting saddle is by behaving badly. Thus twisting from side to side, not 'going forward', a sour attitude, poor performance, bucking, rearing and so on, are all very often signs of pain and fear.

What should I do?

When such problems arise the first things to check are the teeth and mouth, the feet and, of course, the saddle and back. Ideally your saddle should be checked by a qualified saddle fitter before problems show, and certainly before and during your horse's working season to monitor any changes in muscle development and corresponding alterations to the saddle (it might need reflocking). See Useful Addresses, page 150.

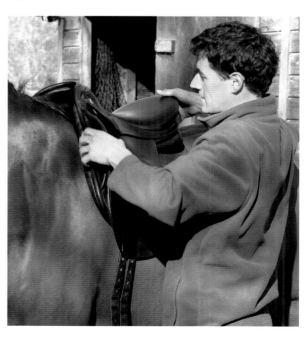

42 Find a bit that suits your horse

There is still an old-fashioned notion that if we find the right bit our horse will be magically transformed and go like a champion. This is not really true, and it is more important to have a well-educated and sensitive pair of hands on the other end of the reins, not to mention a similar seat in the saddle. However, bits *can* make a difference, so let's look at the fundamental requirements.

What is the most important thing to look for in a bit?

There are two vital points that any bit must fulfil:

- it must be comfortable to the horse;
- it must give the rider reasonable control.

There are many horse people who believe that horses should be ridden without a bit, and there are also those who say, quite correctly, that if a horse really wants to 'go' no bit will stop him. This is true, but in an emergency you probably have more chance of control with a bit in his mouth. And since horses are unpredictable and by instinct 'flight' animals, to my mind it is risky for most people to ride in a bitless bridle.

So what should I look for?

There are several new bitting systems today that appear to be helping many horses. In general, look for the mildest bit that will do the job for your particular horse – and hands.

I prefer a bit that follows the contours of a horse's mouth, such as a French link snaffle and a half-moon pelham, depending on the horse. Many horses go very kindly in a pelham, and in training our first aim should be to have a calm, happy and co-operative horse. We can progress to a double bridle later, if required.

Your aim should be a horse who does not – repeat *not* – mouth his

bit a lot and produce quantities of frothy saliva, which is *not* a 'moist mouth' and a horse happily chomping his bit, but indicates a distressed horse. Ideally he should go forwards calmly, happily and lightly. Note also that the production of excess saliva and froth can apparently be due to a slight reaction in the mouth to certain metals, or because the horse does not like the taste of the bit material; a clear indication of this would be if a horse is champing excessively, or obviously looks unhappy. Try rubber and vulcanite to see if the horse finds the taste more acceptable; and if it is not, stainless steel is tasteless. And if you want to give the horse a lasting, pleasant taste, give him a mint before you put on his bridle and ride him. This also encourages the horse to play with, and move his bit around a little, and he then associates taking the bit with a pleasant experience.

Fit and adjustment

The most comfortable and effective, and therefore correct way for bits to fit seems to have been lost down the years. And very often a horse's noseband is nowadays put on too tightly – this is counter-productive because it will prevent the horse opening his mouth a little so that he can comfortably and slightly mouth his bit, something we are all supposed to be aiming for. A bit should be selected and fitted according to the following parameters:

- It should be only so wide as to allow the width of one finger at one side between the bit cheek and the corner of the lips; then it will neither slide about nor pinch.
- Thick bits are not comfortable for some horses, particularly native ponies and cobs (who might also have a thick tongue), Arabs and some Thoroughbreds, all of whom often have a small mouth. A thinner bit may be accepted more readily.
- The correct height for a straightbar snaffle, a Kimblewick or pelham is for it to *comfortably touch* the corners of the mouth, creating *no* wrinkles.
- The correct height for a jointed snaffle or the bridoon of a double bridle is for it to make *one* wrinkle.
- The correct height for the curb bit of a double bridle is for it to lie about 1cm (½in) below the bridoon (thin snaffle), not touching the corners of the mouth at all. You should be able to run one finger comfortably under the curb chain, which should come into effect when the bit cheek forms a 45-degree angle with the line of the lips.
- Don't use a noseband which goes under the bit if the bit has a curb chain. It will interfere with the action of the bit, and be counter productive.

These are established guidelines that have been well proven over centuries. If you are in doubt, try to find a knowledgeable, caring expert to help you along the above lines.

Healthy and happy

43 Try riding with less equipment

There is so much persuasively marketed tack available these days that it is no wonder that tackrooms are bulging with it. Of course, a skilled horseman or woman should be able to ride with just a simple bridle and noseband (if any) and a saddle (if that, some say); but if we are not getting along too well with what we have already, sometimes we look to other equipment to help us.

Gadget or training aid? What's the difference?

Gadgets might be considered as equipment that coerces a horse into assuming a particular posture and way of going, whereas training aids rather suggest to him a posture or way of going to help him get the idea of adopting the desired outline voluntarily. However, this is my own definition, and much depends on how the item is fitted, adjusted and used.

Few people have their horses from foalhood, which is when training should start, and many do not feel able to train and educate a horse.

Most people buy adult horses ready to work, but these often bring with them memories of past bad experiences, which cause them to manifest 'problem behaviour'. The tendency then is to look for a stronger bit, or to hoist it up, or tighten the noseband, or resort to other equipment. However, there are other things that might be considered first.

What should I do?

There is no point in cluttering up a horse with more equipment than he really needs: some people have a real tendency to do this, putting on all sorts of gadgets as a preventative, not a corrective measure – or even without thinking about it. This can

actually create physical discomfort, psychological pressure and consequent behaviour problems.

If problems do arise, go back to basics and try a well-fitting saddle and a comfortable bit – nothing else. Often, increased mental and physical comfort plus confident, sensitive riding will sort out any problem. Of course, it may be necessary to have the horse examined to make sure he is not in pain from a slight injury, has dental trouble or is suffering from poor feet or shoeing. Lessons from a sympathetic teacher (see next topic, page 67) who has an understanding of equine behaviour and biomechanics, or from a remedial trainer, will then usually find the cause of a problem.

44 Find a sympathetic teacher

The relationship between a horse, rider and teacher is a sort of eternal triangle, because learning can go on for ever, and all three parties in the relationship are equally important. Many people try several teachers before finding one they feel comfortable with, and whom they trust. How should you feel about your teacher, and what should you look for?

Where do I start?

If you prefer a particular discipline of equestrianism, your administering organization may have a list or directory of teachers who should be able to teach you how to progress in it. A good way to find a compatible teacher is by word of mouth so you can quiz whoever is doing the recommending. Regional horse magazines have advertisements for teachers so you can ring them and judge carefully from your conversation whether you feel you will get on.

Always check that the teacher has third party liability insurance and comply with it yourself: you will probably have to wear a properly secured hard hat up to the latest approved standards, your horse will have to be healthy and sound, and you should try to do what the teacher says unless you have doubts, in which case discuss them. If you do something against the teacher's instructions and have an accident, it's not his or her fault.

Your first lessons with a new teacher

The first thing to note is your teacher's attitude to horses: kindness, firmness, patience and fairness are much more humane and effective than unreasonably forceful tactics. Note his or her assessment of your horse and see if it makes sense, even if it's not exactly like yours. Although your teacher at this stage is not, and may never become, a personal friend, you should feel a measure of understanding and caring about you and your horse, and you should find him or her easy to talk to. Note also your horse's reaction to the methods used, whether or not the teacher rides your horse, and above all, relax and follow your hunches.

Give the teacher a chance to help you – but if, after a few sessions, you are not happy, be honest, and say so politely, and look elsewhere if you cannot sort things out. This is ultimately best for all of you.

45 Discover your 'horse intuition'

The subject of innately understanding horses is one that many people find difficult to comprehend. Is it something you either have or you haven't, or is it something that can be cultivated? I believe that it can be cultivated *if* you are a sensitive and sensible person. However, obviously you must like horses and not be in it merely for the prestige, and you must be prepared for lifelong learning.

The natural ...

Some people are so tuned in to horses that you get the impression they must have been a horse in a previous life. They just seem to fully understand horses and their circumstances naturally, even horses they don't know, and they always seem to know what to do for the best in any situation. Despite the fact that horses are big, strong and potentially dangerous animals, these

people never panic or get cross, and horses just seem to 'go' for them: they can often be seen to relax in their presence, turn their attention to them, and actually watch calmly for their lead.

... and the acquired

That description may also apply to certain people who were not born with such good fortune but who have

acquired their 'feel' for horses through remaining open-minded, perceptive and genuinely caring about horses. The sort of people who are 'in horses' for the kudos that horses always bring, the chance to *win* and bask in the reflected glory of the horse, will probably never acquire horse intuition, because they do not have the right attitude to do so.

A few decades ago there were two superb horsemen competing on the home and international circuits.

One (let's call him A) was generally regarded as a natural, and the other (B) as having acquired the necessary skills through dedication, commitment and the open-mindedness to learn all he could. They were both quiet, brave riders who each for many years represented their country.

I mention this to show that it is possible to become as good as the naturals even if you are not one of them. On one occasion A made a basic error coming into a fence which B had cleared faultlessly, and the commentator said that it was because he did not always analyse what to do, relying on instinct, whereas the other had it all worked out in minute detail. However, in another competition A won because B had miscalculated his timing.

How can I become more intuitive with horses?

- Spend as much time as you can with horses, any horses, observing and getting a feel for them, under all sorts of circumstances.
- Try not to be always in a rush to get done and get away from the stables. Most of us are pressured for time these days – and our horses know it. They know that there is no point trying to communicate or setting up 'together time' because you are not really 'connected' at that moment: your mind is half elsewhere even as you talk to your horse, stroke him, feed him, even ride him. This is no good. When you are with your horse by all means keep an eye on the time if you have to, but think about *him*, not where you are going next, and you will then be surprised what comes to you from him. Spend time sitting in his field or box reading, or just being with him.
- It is also important to spend time just standing or sitting quietly and observing horses, both where they

cannot see you and where they can. Try to 'open' your spirit to them and allow a feeling to come to you for each horse.
- Finally, go and learn as much as you possibly can from books, lecture/ demonstrations, talks and courses, videos and DVDs. Go to shows, competitions and to other people's stables; try to assess each horse's personality and immediate feelings on your considered first impression. It will often be right.
- It is also particularly important to

learn about the 'body language' of horses so that you can recognize on a practical level what a horse is feeling – if he is happy, sad, frightened, confident, relaxed, sick or in pain, depressed, worried and anxious or content and happy.

One day, not too far hence if you are open-minded and genuinely want to know, you will find that you can 'do it', too, and some horse, somewhere, sometime, may be very relieved that you can.

46 Recognize what makes your horse happy

Believe it or not, it has only just started to be recognized formally that horses can be happy: their emotions have long been a contentious point among horsemen, scientists, behavioural therapists and trainers. Many other people, on the other hand, have never been able to understand how anyone could think that humans can have emotions but animals cannot.

How can I tell if a horse is happy?

I have always thought of animals as souls or spirits like us, but inside a differently shaped body. Having been brought up with various animals, I took it for granted that they were like us with the same basic needs. It was only the details that mattered – for instance, you would not give a horse a bone to chew, or a dog a bucket of oats. To recognize happiness when you see it you have to understand horse body language, and it can be very subtle. There is an air of joyful energy or, conversely, contented relaxation: in the first the ears will be pricked sharply, the nostrils somewhat flared, the eyes bright and confident, and the gait animated. In the second, the ears will be rather to the side, loose, the eyes soft, full and either interested or sleepy, and the body toned but relaxed.

So what makes horses happy?

A horse is made happy by the same things that make any animal happy – feeling comfortable and safe. Thus to be happy, horses need:
- enough suitable food and water;
- congenial company, normally and preferably equine;
- shelter from extremes of weather, and somewhere peaceful and dry to lie and rest;
- space to move around at various gaits, to lie down, roll and get up easily, and to escape harassment from unfriendly herdmates;
- the facility for movement on reasonable ground conditions to satisfy their inborn need to be almost constantly gently walking about, with occasional bursts at a faster speed.

These are the basic daily needs an owner can cater for; others are needed less often, such as veterinary care and farriery. Provide all these fundamentals, and your horse is very likely to be truly, horsily happy.

47 Behave towards your horse in a way he'll understand

Horses are praised (rewarded) and reprimanded (corrected) constantly in a free herd: if they were not, they would never learn equine manners and mores. Learning how horses deal with each other helps us to adopt the same language or communication system to get through to them, whether or not we are happy with what they are doing.

The horses' own language

There are many ways of training, schooling, educating and teaching horses. All systems aim at helping us to get horses to do what we want them to do, and to not do what we don't want them to do. So far so good – but how exactly do we do that?

Watch horses together and you will see two main types of communication that meet these requirements:

- When a horse does something to another which the latter does not like, this one will nip, bite or kick the first. As well as a reprimand, these also mean 'get away'.
- When a horse does something to another which the latter likes, he allows the first horse to remain in his space and may rub smoothly against him, as in mutual grooming with the upper lip and teeth on the withers and back of the first.

We have a well-developed facility to praise or reprimand horses, which they also have, but we don't use it very much: the voice. We can reprimand with a short, sharp sound (like a sharp nip or kick), usually the word 'no' in a disapproving tone and with squared-up body stance. We can praise with a smooth, pleasant sound, like mutual grooming, usually the words 'good boy' in a soothing, pleased tone plus relaxed posture. Horses understand both these sounds almost magically, from the ground or in the saddle, if they are said consistently and in the right way. The tone is everything.

Praise can also be shown, again from the ground or saddle, by firmly and slowly rubbing the withers, back or shoulder, to replace another horse's muzzle. Firm patting and thumping are not horse-language for 'all right' because they feel like bites and kicks – short, sharp and unpleasant – and are exactly the opposite of what you mean. Stroking is clear, meaningful and positive.

71

48 Learn your horse's language

Horses' main means of communicating with each other is by what we often call 'body language'. They use body positions, postures, facial expressions and the positions of the ears and tail to tell each other and us how they are feeling and what they mean. These attitudes can be quite plain or extremely subtle, and different combinations mean different things.

The importance of understanding horses

For what is supposed to be a two-way partnership, the communication between horse and rider has long been very one-sided in most cases. A common point of view has been that the horse is expected to behave well and be an uncomplaining, undemanding servant to man. Even when many people do talk to horses, it is usually to tell them off for something, rather than to praise them. When horses do something well, most people just accept it; but when they do something wrong or badly, these same people are quick to correct them.

There have always been more sensitive and outgoing horsemasters who have readily assessed what a horse has been 'saying', and have perhaps changed their plans or actions accordingly. There are some who can just sense how a horse is feeling – and this ability can come with experience and open-mindedness.

How can I learn?

Most books on equine behaviour contain pictures of horse body language with captions explaining what the different postures and attitudes mean, and all of them are well worth studying (see Further Reading, page 150). These should start you off if you are unfamiliar with equine body language, but it is important to apply the pictures to real horses as often as you can, so that recognition becomes second nature to you.

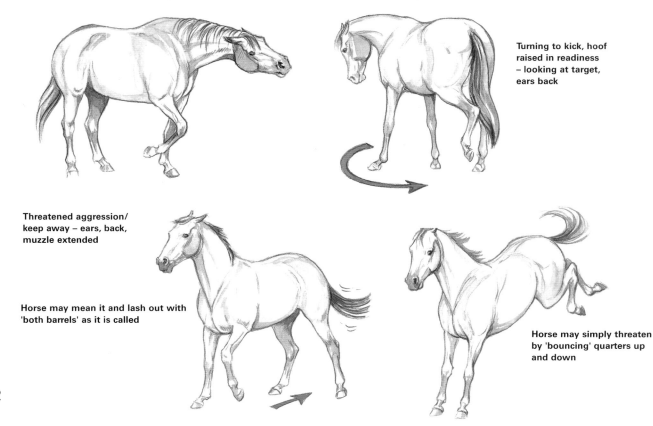

Turning to kick, hoof raised in readiness – looking at target, ears back

Threatened aggression/ keep away – ears, back, muzzle extended

Horse may mean it and lash out with 'both barrels' as it is called

Horse may simply threaten by 'bouncing' quarters up and down

Reading the signals: facial expressions

Extended top lip indicates pleasure

Anxiety – mouth and lips tight, eyes worried

Annoyance – ears back, nostrils wrinkled up and back

Discomfort or pain – nostrils 'sucked in' above, muzzle tight

Relaxed/dozy

Alert and ready to flee

Defending self against something in front

Herding posture – get out of my space

Tail swishing or thrashing and head turned towards something irritating

49 Explore complementary/ alternative therapies

There is no doubt that your vet should be your first thought when there is anything wrong with your horse, but complementary therapies can be very effective, and certainly merit investigation. They can be used alone, or to complement (hence the name) orthodox medicine, and you can often apply them yourself, usually after a consultation with a trained therapist.

How do they work?

There are many complementary therapies of different types, most of them aiming to encourage the body to heal itself by stimulating healing energies in different ways. Orthodox medicine, conversely, usually works by giving the body back-up and support with drugs, antibiotics and so on. Therefore therapies of different types can often be used together, with or without orthodox medicine.

Where do I start?

In order to use a therapy most effectively, I believe that owners should use a trained therapist or practitioner at least for the first consultation, and then as ongoing support, depending on the condition. Many remedies, from feed supplements to physiotherapy machines, are on sale to the general public with sometimes the briefest of instructions.

You should first of all contact your vet and/or a trained therapist with a view to discussing the matter and obtaining a referral ('permission') from the vet for a complementary therapist to treat the horse. In the UK and certain other countries only vets are allowed to diagnose horses' illnesses and injuries, but the two should consult together about your horse and bring you into the discussions. There are homoeopathic veterinary surgeons, but few vets are qualified as herbalists or in other therapies. No reputable therapist would treat an animal without a veterinary referral. Here are details of some of the more effective therapies:

Herbalism: Surely the oldest therapy in the world: food and medicine from plants have been sought out by humans and other creatures since life began. Herbal medicines work by providing substances that will counteract disorders and stimulate the immune system to fight disease. It uses substances found in plants to clear the body's energy

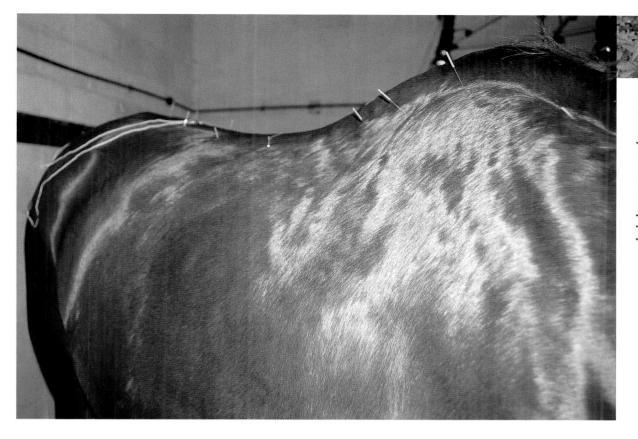

channels and allow energy to flow freely again, clearing toxins, pathogens (germs) and general debris. Remedies are mainly given in the feed, although creams and lotions can be used. Herbalism can help most problems, both physical and psychological.

Homoeopathy: Homoeopathy treats the patient's individual traits, rather than the disease or disorder currently present. Homoeopaths regard disease symptoms as expressions of disharmony in the patient, and believe that once harmony is restored the symptoms and disorder will disappear. This is why two different horses suffering from the same problem may be given different remedies. Homoeopathic remedies come from animal, vegetable and mineral sources and are given by mouth, although there are homoeopathic ointments and other products.

Acupuncture, acupressure and Shiatsu: These three therapies are closely related and work by the stimulation of free energy flow along channels or meridians believed to run throughout the body. Acupuncture stimulates specific points along these meridians by the use of needles; acupressure does the same by finger pressure; but Shiatsu uses mainly finger pressure along the accessible parts of the whole meridian. Again, the idea is that blocked, or depleted, or excess energy in one part of a meridian or meridians causes an uneven flow

of energy and so ill-health. Again, the whole individual and his or her traits are treated to help in just about any condition you can think of, mental or physical. Shiatsu also employs gentle movements, stretches and rotations to promote the 'feel-good' factor and encourage spontaneous natural healing, including stimulation of the immune system.

Aromatherapy: This therapy treats bodily and mental ailments using essential oils from plants. Again, the rationale is to treat the individual and stimulate self-healing. The oils can be rubbed on to the body or inhaled. Aromas are actually physical in nature. Minute particles are given off by certain substances and are carried on the air, breathed in by the person or animal, and then dissolve in the moisture of the mucous membranes, and so may find their way into the body fluids such as lymph and blood. Horses seem to respond particularly well to aromatherapy.

Osteopathy: This is a healing art and science aimed at resolving painful conditions caused by misalignments of the skeleton. The practitioner adjusts muscles and joints which are perpetuating the misalignment with a view to correcting it. Many people and animals regarded as permanently incapacitated have been restored to health and fitness by means of osteopathy. For some aspects of osteopathy, horses need sedating, for which a veterinary surgeon is also needed.

50 Try massage and stretching

Massage and stretching are fairly simple techniques, which any intelligent, sensitive owner can learn to a basic level sufficient to help their horse. There are whole books available about them, and any conscientious therapist should be prepared to show clients suitable techniques to help keep their horses toned up and supple, and to improve their comfort during work.

What are their benefits?

The body is a dynamic structure, and because it is on the move so much and is so complex, it can suffer from small, unnoticed injuries, which can escalate. Athletic demands can cause, among other injuries, small muscle over-stretches or tears. The body's natural reaction is to clamp up the muscles around it to protect it from movement and further injury; these muscle tissues may then go into spasm and 'knot' or shorten. The horse may then start moving in an unnatural way (compensatory movement), which can cause further muscle problems.

Gentle manipulations such as massage and stretching help to 'loosen up' these areas, and encourage suppleness and the restoration of normal use. Both techniques can also be used as 'preventive' methods, to gently loosen up a horse before work and get the blood and energy flowing through his tissues; and they help to maintain a brisk circulation after work, to remove toxins and tissue debris, and to even out any little spasms that may be forming. Again, several books have been written on these techniques (*see* Further Reading, page 150).

Here I should like to describe the basic massage techniques known as effleurage and tapotment, and the sorts of stretches that can be safely administered by a sensible owner.

'Effleurage' is similar to firm stroking, and horses enjoy it, once they are used to it. It is used to relax a horse after work, or to get his muscles moving and responding before work. It is used all over the body with flat, relaxed hands on muscle masses in the direction of the hair; the legs are stroked firmly upwards.

Place your hands on a muscular area; start away from the central body area and gradually work the areas closer to the heart. Lean your weight on to the horse with firm arms and slightly bent elbows, and push your hands along the muscles, lighten up and keep your hands on the horse as you bring them back, and repeat the action.

'Tapotment' is a percussive, stimulating technique and can be done with the hands in a roof (cupped) shape, 'clapping' up and down with alternate hands, or 'hacking' with the little-finger edges of the hands, again on muscular areas. This bounces muscle tissue into action and moves blood, lymph and energy through it.

Never massage any injured area directly, but maybe do so (on advice) *very gently* around an injury to help disperse swelling (congested fluid). Do not massage horses suffering from systemic diseases (such as influenza), pregnant mares, or if you do not seem to be helping a horse. Always be ready to consult your therapist if in doubt or having problems.

Stretching

Simple stretches can be performed before work on the legs and neck, and after work to even up any tension or to relax muscles that have worked and may be slightly tense or contracted from fatigue.

To stretch the forelegs, stand facing the tail and pick up the foot as for picking out. For the left leg, have your right hand under the knee and your left under the fetlock to support the leg comfortably. Stand with your left leg behind you to take your weight, and your right leg a little in front so that you have a safe, wide base of support. Gently draw the leg forwards, keeping the hoof low and leaning back on your left leg. Don't pull, keep it comfortable, and put the foot down when you've finished – do not let the horse snatch it away and drop it. To stretch the leg back slightly, keep the forearm vertical at first with your left hand under the knee and your right under the fetlock. With your weight on your right leg, keep the hoof close to the ground and carefully stretch the leg straight back. Reverse the instructions for the right leg.

To stretch the hind legs, stand facing the tail with the same stance and pick up the left foot. Have your right hand under the hock and your left under the fetlock. Leaning on your left leg, gently ask the horse to stretch the leg forwards, return it and then put the foot down. To stretch the leg back slightly, pick up the foot, have your left hand placed on the front of the hock and your right on the front of the fetlock, and ask the horse to move the leg back a little by placing your weight on your right leg. Allow the leg to return, and put the foot down.

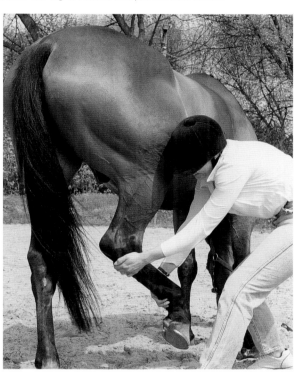

To stretch the neck, place the horse alongside the wall or fence and ask him to reach round towards you for a carrot, held only so far along his side as to be comfortable for him at first. Give him the carrot at once. Repeat on the other side. Then squat down and pass the carrot up between his forelegs, bringing it down and back a little to get him to stretch his topline.

To do the *complementary stretch upwards*, stand close to one side, in front of his shoulder with your back to his tail, with the heels of your hands under and behind his round jawbones. Gently persuade him by pushing carefully to raise his head and nose in the air, then slowly release.

Always talk reassuringly to the horse, and only do what he can achieve comfortably. He will soon become quite expert at stretches.

51 Enhance your horse's feel-good factor

We all want to feel comfortable and safe and also good about ourselves, and the practical ways of doing this have already been discussed; but what about other, less mundane ways of making your horse feel good? Horses are very sensitive creatures, and undoubtedly there are many people who do not realize just how much they are 'tuned in' to the attitudes and feelings of the humans they come in contact with.

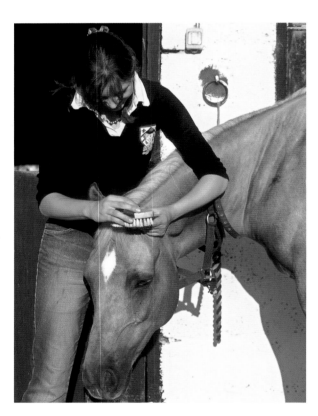

The inner horse

If you have ever been associated with people who looked after your physical needs, but paid little attention to your mental, psychological or spiritual ones, you will know how hurtful and lonely this can feel. Horses are very capable of feeling lonely and excluded from those who are physically closest to them, such as an owner who uses them rather than really cares about them, or a herd of other horses who will not let them join their family.

This can also apply to horses kept largely away from normal contact with others, such as in stables where they can only see and hear each other, but not smell or touch. Normal social contact at liberty with others is important

to their happiness, and *especially* being with their chosen friends. The 'traditional' practice of separating friends so that they do not form 'impossible' bonds is unfair and totally unsympathetic, and is calculated to make horses feel distressed and lonely.

Spending time with your horse makes him feel wanted, loved and important, but you can use the time to do pleasant things with him, which will promote good feelings. Take your time over giving him a thorough, old-fashioned grooming in a relaxed and reassuring way. Learn to give him a basic Shiatsu treatment yourself: horses obviously find its effects absolutely blissful!

Keep your horse's surroundings conducive to horse security and comfort. In his stable, for instance, do your best to ensure that he has more than one outlook to a view. Give him as large a box as you can, have him next to his friends, keep the box well ventilated but draught free, see that there is always clean water available for him, and several kinds of forage for variety. Very importantly, see that his bedding is kept not only clean but also *dry* – and I repeat, dry.

Finally, do everything you possibly can to secure some decent, year-round turnout for your horse – with his friends.

52 Teach your horse to accept medicines

There are times when our horse has to have something objectionable administered in order to achieve something beneficial, such as maintaining his good health. Worming medicines, antibiotics, phenylbutazone and other medicines are never welcome, but some horses make a real fuss about them – and many people are driven to distraction by this behaviour. What is the best way to handle this frustrating problem?

When needs must

If a horse's medicine is essential, you may need to get your veterinary surgeon to administer it, possibly under sedation. In most cases, however, the horse can be controlled and gradually taught co-operative behaviour by sufficient confident, knowledgeable handling, and pleasant rewards for good behaviour, long before the time comes to get the medicine down him.

Administering phenylbutazone: In order to persuade your horse to take 'bute in his feed, keep the powder sachets in the freezer or fridge, because if they are really cold, the bitter taste is greatly reduced. A small caravan-type fridge in your bay at the livery yard would serve this purpose, or take them to the yard wrapped in bubble wrap to keep them cold and give the dose in a small feed full of goodies on arrival. Another way is to cream the powder in water and syringe it in.

Administering wormers or medicines in a syringe: Do the job as quickly, quietly and craftily as you can. Have the syringe ready with the plunger pulled out and held behind your back, give the horse a mint to distract him, then calmly put one hand over his face to steady his head and slip the syringe *all the way into the corner of his mouth pointing back to his throat*, and press it quickly. Accustom your horse to syringes by keeping an old one and syringing in molasses, honey, carrot juice and so on, so he never knows what's coming. If you think he can smell wormer, dip the end of the syringe in treacle first.

Make a sandwich: Mixing various medicines with minty toothpaste on a sandwich often goes down well, but check with your vet that this will not affect the efficacy of the medicine. Always be calm, firm and positive, and praise and reward your horse immediately after he has taken his medicine.

Handling your horse

Coming to hand

There is a common belief that if you are not confident in the saddle you can concentrate on groundwork alone, because it is easier and safer. However, this latter assumption is not true! What *is* true is that groundwork can have an immense effect on the horse's other work under saddle or in harness, although this does not seem to be fully appreciated by some. Thus if you have a poor relationship with a horse from the ground, sitting on him won't generally improve matters. As in many things there are exceptions to this, but usually you need to gain a horse's trust and establish mutual respect from the ground if you want his other work to be rewarding and enjoyable for both of you.

Handling horses well is extremely important, not least for safety reasons. Compare the horse's body and mind with those of the human. It is said that around 80 per cent of horse owners and riders are young to middle-aged adult females, many of whom will have an average weight of, say, roughly 10 stones (140lb or 63kg), whereas the average riding horse may weigh half a ton or tonne. Humans normally do not take fright and charge off in a panic away from anything they find remotely frightening – whereas horses normally do, left to their own devices. If they are aggressive their sheer weight, not to mention their propensity to bite and kick, makes them a formidable physical opponent for a human; whereas humans, by comparison, would be quite helpless against horses. So from the ground there is no contest – unless we employ certain psychological techniques together with some helpful basic equipment, to make the horse think that we are at least an equal partner, and – as many would have it – preferably superior to him.

Ideally, horses would be handled correctly from their first days in this world so that their further training or education could progress logically from being an already well-mannered, socially experienced and 'people-aware' young horse; but even on professional studs these days, this is often not the case. Today's difficult economic conditions are blamed – but even if this were so, I believe that breeders who sell poorly handled or unhandled youngsters are failing in their responsibility not only to their customers and the horse world in general, but to the horses they breed. Certainly there are enough bad-mannered horses around these days.

I hope that the information and suggestions given in this section will give readers food for thought, and at least somewhere to start if they are faced with a horse that is difficult to handle.

53 Be your horse's leader or supporter

There are arguments about whether horses need or provide each other with leadership as we know it. They undoubtedly follow other horses' examples and younger ones almost always look to older ones for this and defer to them. They learn, in time, that their elders usually know best. Timid horses also rely on confident ones for 'advice'.

How to be your horse's leader

To be your horse's leader, you must generally be:

- Calm and quiet – so that your horse feels that there is nothing around to be afraid of.
- Firm – because you are firm and neither wishy-washy nor brutal you convey confidence and safety, which horses find comforting.

- Positive – because you are positive the horse feels that you are in control of the situation and he can rely on you.

There are other necessary qualities such as:

- Gentleness and kindness, with firmness.
- Empathy so that you can see and feel your horse's viewpoint.
- Technical knowledge, which you can acquire from books, lessons and courses, so that you know what you are doing.
- Judgement which should come from correct experience.
- The right attitude which combines all of the above.

Can we aim for equal partnerships with our horses?

My personal answer is 'almost'. Based on many years of experience and observation, I believe that we should aim for a near-equal 51:49 partnership in our favour.

Getting the balance right

Some feel that we should build a mutually beneficial relationship with a horse based on consideration, trust, respect, confidence and so on, in order that one partner does not have the upper hand. Conversely, others feel that horses must always be subservient to us, showing obedience and submission (a word that still appears on some dressage test mark sheets). In fact, many traditionalists still describe a horse as 'a good servant' which conveys that the horse 'knows who's boss'.

In my opinion neither of these viewpoints are conducive to achieving a good and safe relationship with horses. Even though some feel that the use of the word 'leadership' is

inappropriate, I cannot think of a better one to convey what horses need from us – confidence, education, assertiveness, empathy, protection, firmness, positiveness, direction, guidance, stimulation and mutual respect (among others). There are many qualities there but they are all invaluable in dealing effectively, and fairly, with horses.

In my experience there is room for give and take in most horse-human relationships but, when the situation demands, horses must do as we ask. Horses are born into a society alien to them; they are not capable of making decisions in life or death predicaments such as traffic. Consider this: horses will always think like the prey animals they are. When startled their first instinct is to shy or gallop off first and maybe think later. The average riding horse weighs half a ton and can get from nought to 30mph in three or four seconds with no thought for where he is going or for anyone on or near him. Do you really want to be on that and not have 'the upper hand'? This is where your one per cent is vital.

My firm view is that horses not only need *good* leadership but also that most actually want it.

So what's the answer?

There are many people around today, of many persuasions, who can help you to educate your horse and socialize him to a human society. I find that more and more horses and ponies have not had this start in life. The best people will also teach you how to go on, will never abuse or beat up your horse, or tell you to, and will listen to the opinions and questions you have.

54 Earn your horse's trust

Trust is important to all animals, including humans. If you are with someone you don't trust, you feel alone or even frightened. Horses live in herds and usually have at least one friend or other horse they trust, such as a parent or senior herd member. Domestic horses quite often do their work on their own but with us, so trust is crucial.

Equine personalities

The problem with many ill-treated or poorly handled horses, or horses that have not been handled at all, is that they have never had cause to trust humans. Even if they do not actually mistrust us, they may know little about us because no one has bothered to get to know them, to handle them, or to teach them the basics of human/horse standards, manners and social interaction.

Horses that are not naturally outgoing and self-confident, but rather look to others for what to do, for guidance and protection, can quickly become fearful and defensive in unfamiliar or worrying situations, and this is potentially dangerous for all concerned. On the other hand, those who *are* braver and self-assured may 'try us out' to see how easily we can be intimidated – although I have come across some like this who seem to feel *so* superior that any kind of domination appears unnecessary to them unless they are treated badly.

The best ways to gain trust

There is no doubt that horses respond best to humans who are self-confident and – as always! – calm, firm and positive. They prefer people who do not cause them discomfort, pain or fear, who provide guidance when appropriate, and who will reliably look after their needs – and they do understand all this.

Whatever you do with your horse, if you can avoid hurting, worrying or frightening him, he will trust you and feel safe with you, and what you ask of him; he will even put up with a certain amount of discomfort such as farriery, veterinary or dental treatment because he knows that basically his life and the people in it are fine. Horses like this actively look to humans they know and trust when there is trouble with them or in the herd, even coming to seek help. This is a massive compliment to their owner's horse skills and attitude.

55 Teach your horse to be handled all over

Every horse should learn to allow himself to be handled all over, as long as the handler treats him with respect and sympathy. This is one of the most fundamental requirements in his education, and most important for essential care procedures, including veterinary, farriery and dental treatment. Many horses, though, don't always tolerate these latter procedures, usually due to lack of education or to bad experiences in the past.

Making up for the past

If you acquire a horse who will not readily allow himself to be handled and is already fully grown and perhaps 'set in his ways', your inclination may be to manage and work around his behaviour, rather than trying to retrain him. However, although this is understandable, it is far better to try and improve matters if at all possible, than to simply hedge round the problems (which is tantamount to avoiding them).

The main problem with not fully addressing the issue is that some horses will then start being difficult over other things as well, because they have learnt that you won't persist, and will let them 'get away with it'. Therefore quite quickly you will have a growing catalogue of 'no-go' areas and a very difficult horse.

What can I do?

The following two methods are often successful:

a) to retrain the horse, rewarding him *instantly* when he shows the slightest improvement in allowing his body to be handled;

b) to gradually persist in handling him safely only stopping and instantly praising him when he permits it.

a) Ideally, have a competent helper who is not frightened to hold the horse, maybe in a bridle or nose chain, whilst you try the 'forbidden' handling. Speak confidently to the horse, and at the slightest improvement *instantly* stop and say 'good boy' in an approving tone. Repeat the process a few times then wait for another day.

b) Have a stick about 3ft (1m) long and fasten a stuffed glove or soft pad to the end of it. Standing well out of reach of teeth or hooves, gradually stroke the horse with the glove, getting nearer the out-of-bounds area, praising any improvement, as above. Do not pussyfoot around, do not tickle, tease, hurt or provoke the horse. Do not stop the contact until he stops objecting.

Basically, reassure the horse vocally saying 'eeeeeasy' or 'aaaaall right', say a confident 'no' when he objects, and only say 'gooood boy' and stop the process when some improvement is shown, however slight.

56 Teach your horse to pick up a foot willingly

Horses are naturally protective of their head and their feet. Their head, obviously, contains their brain and vital sensory organs and they instinctively protect them, and their feet are their only means of escape, flight and security. In the wild, a horse lying down on the ground is very vulnerable, which is why they spend most of the time on their feet.

Preliminaries

It is always much easier to pick up the feet of a horse who is thoroughly accustomed to being handled all over, so make sure that this has been done (see page 85). Because his feet will need trimming by a farrier about every six weeks, this task is one that must not be delayed if you have a horse who does not co-operate.

A horse is usually reluctant to pick up his feet because he has not been trained to do so as a specific lesson, or because he has been hurt, roughly handled, or frightened during the process. Current injury or arthritis are also reasons. Have the horse standing comfortably and well balanced, more or less four square, so that it is easy for him to stand on three legs.

How do I do it?

Although it is easier for the horse to pick up a hind foot, many make more fuss over their hind than their fore feet.

- Stand by a leg facing his tail, and put the hand nearest to him gently and confidently on his shoulder or hip. Stroke him and run your leg down to the fetlock.
- Lean into him a little to push him over to his other side. If he leans against you, say a firm 'no' and carry on if safe.

- For a front leg, press behind his knee with your elbow. Pinch his tendons just above the fetlock and say 'up' as you hold or pull gently but confidently on the fetlock at the ergot.
- When the foot comes up, hold it momentarily under the toe with the joints bent so that it is uncomfortable for him to put weight on it, praise him, then put the foot down in a controlled way. Don't hold it up too high.
- If he stamps it down, say 'no'. Repeat once, and praise him.
- Someone giving him titbits immediately he does the right thing reinforces your praise.

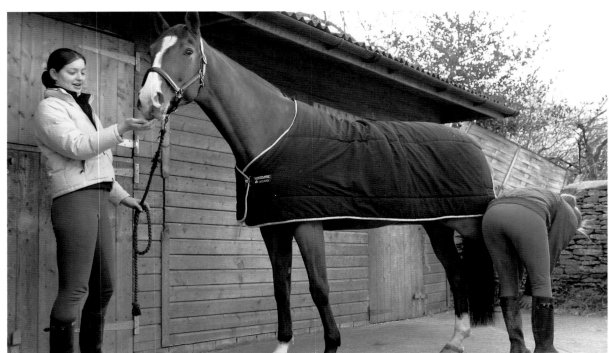

57 Teach your horse to stand for the farrier

Increasingly, farriers and vets do not appear to be taught enough about handling horses and ponies, unlike 'the old days'. If a vet has to deal with an animal that is obviously difficult, he or she can give it a sedative; a farrier, however, does not have this option, so many will not take on horses that are difficult to deal with – they have enough work already.

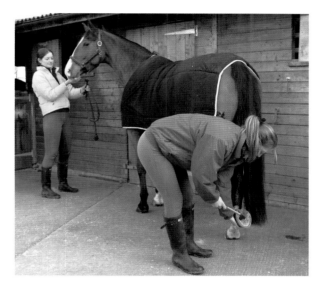

The right farrier

Part of the solution to this problem (assuming that the horse will actually pick up his feet in the first place – see page 86) is to find a farrier who works in a way that you like: who is not rough, who does not hold the horse's leg up too high or, in particular, out at an unnatural angle – which can hurt, unbalance and frighten the horse – and who has a Professional (note the capital P) attitude to his work. A little patience, and horse sense go a very long way. A farrier without these qualities can turn a horse into a difficult customer with just one untoward incident.

How can I help?

- As obedience is basically the owner's responsibility, it is important to practise at home. Using the usual technique of praise ('good boy') and titbits when he is good, and correction ('no') when he resists, plus persistent, firm but gentle insistence, the horse can be taught to hold his foot up for you for increasingly long periods of time.
- Gradually hold the foot and leg as the farrier would, at similar angles forwards and backwards, and for longer

periods of time; and get a tripod, and support the foot on it as for finishing off. Tap and scrape the foot or shoe with a hammer or hoofpick.
- Calmly expect the horse to co-operate, use praise and correction instantly when the horse behaves well or otherwise, and have someone else present to give treats the instant the horse is good. This associates the action in the horse's mind with something pleasant – but it has to be at the right moment, or it is pointless, and only makes the owner feel good.

58 Teach your horse to tie up, and to ground tie

Few things cause more trouble than a horse who won't be tied up. It is actually basic manners, but there are many who won't stand for it. Because retraining a full-grown horse can be fraught with problems, many remain like this all their lives; it is also one of those problems which it is not always possible to cure.

Why does it start?

This fault develops because the horse has been tied up and been able to break free when he has pulled back, either due to sheer strength, or when tied to a breakable piece of string on the tie-ring. It also develops when a horse of any age has had a fright when tied up.

How can I help?

Before you start training or retraining, the horse must be amenable to being

handled all over, he should lead and stand well and obey voice commands. He should lower his head on request (see page 90). It is a good plan to pad the headpiece of the headcollar. You can also use a strong fabric or leather neck-collar to which the rope is attached and threaded down through the headcollar jaw ring ; any decent saddler could make one for you. Also, work on a soft surface.

- First, pass the rope through the metal tie-ring and back to the hand of the trainer.
- Hold the long lead (say, a half-length lungeing rein) in one hand, and then groom or stroke the horse with the other hand.
- If he moves away, he can be 'played' on the rein by a sensitive handler, and brought back constantly by saying 'walk on' and 'stand' till he stands by the ring quietly.
- Eventually he learns to move forwards, not backwards, when he feels tension on the rope and his poll, *i.e.* moving away from the pressure, not into it.
- Always praise him the instant he walks forwards and releases the tension.
- If he moves, keep bringing him back, saying 'walk on' and 'stand', then praising him.
- This technique helps many horses, and from here it is an easy step to tying up. However, if he genuinely panics the rope can be lengthened and/or the horse freed.

To work in an enclosed space with a

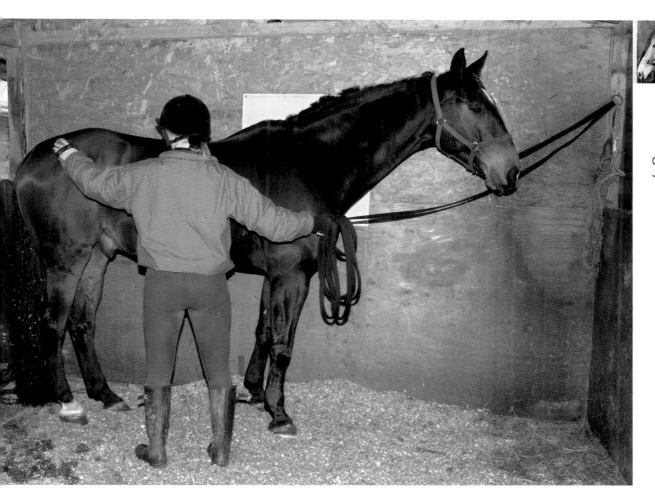

horse who needs to feel reasonably free, thread a double-length lead rope (no clips) through the jaw ring of his headcollar and tuck both ends into your waistband as you work. This gives him a feeling of loose restraint which is often enough to get him to stand still. The rope will not only pull out of your waistband if the horse pulls on it enough, but also, if he treads on one end it will pull through the headcollar ring and fall harmlessly on the floor. If a rope is clipped to his headcollar and he stands on it, he could bring himself down and fall on you as well.

Can I retrain my own horse?

Possibly, but you may feel a good deal more confident with a sympathetic professional to help you, as this problem can be tricky to deal with. It is easier to retrain horses who do this in a fearless way: those who actually panic when tied are much more difficult and dangerous due to memories of something terrifying happening whilst they have been tied up.

To tie a horse up and leave him to fight it out is a barbaric and very dangerous practice: I know of horses that have been seriously injured and killed in this way. If the handlers remain close by, they can approach and correct or pacify the horse, then leave him again, still tied, till he realizes that going forward away from the pressure relieves it. He should not be tied up like this for longer than half an hour. The object is to teach him that he cannot get away: it is *not* to hurt and terrify him. Abusing a horse from behind with a stick or whip is not acceptable either party, because he then learns to kick or sit down, not walk forwards.

Ground tying

It is useful to teach a horse that is good to tie up to stand when the reins or rope are dropped down in front of him to the ground. This is useful in many handling and riding (or falling off) situations.

- Start by tying him to a heavy fallen tree trunk, then a progressively lighter one until he is 'tied' to nothing.
- Stay with him and command 'stand'.
- If he moves, say 'stand' and bring him back. Praise him when he is good.
- Do not go too far away until he is reliable in this technique.
- A refinement is to have a tie-ring fixed firmly to the trunk so that you can use a long rein passing through it, as above.

89

59 Teach your horse to lower his head

It is extremely useful if your horse will lower his head on request, particularly if you are small and he is tall. It is particularly helpful when bridling, grooming, clipping and trimming, calming a horse down, and in the course of veterinary and dental work. Also, if a horse that is frightened and throwing his head up in the air will relax and lower it for you, it shows that he really trusts you.

Signals from the head

We often hear that a horse's 'balancing pole' is his head and neck, and that these are the equivalent to our arms. Horses cannot move easily without free movement of their head, and they cannot see properly if their head is held down, as it would be in some restrictive methods of riding.

If a horse throws his head up, snorting, with ears pricked and nostrils flaring, it is a sign that he is startled or frightened – and other horses will usually 'catch' this feeling, too. But if we can bring the poll voluntarily and freely down below the withers, the horse will quickly calm down.

How can I teach him this?

Have him in an ordinary headcollar and leadrope, and hold him in one hand with a treat in the other. Let him smell the treat, then bend down, lowering the treat down under his nose and saying 'head down' all at the same time. As you do this, also give quick, but not harsh, downward pulls on the leadrope in a pull-and-release fashion.

The instant you get the slightest response, release the pressure say 'gooood boy' in a pleased tone and give him the treat at once. Repeat once and try again some time later. Make it a habit each time you visit your horse.

- Most horses will lower their heads if you bend down and point to the ground, saying 'head down' and giving intermittent pulls on the rope – or, once he is more used to this, the reins of his bridle.
- Next, the horse should respond when free if you say 'head down' and maybe bend and point to the floor.
- Praise can soon take the place of the treat, and you can use the verbal command under saddle to help the horse understand giving to the bit and going with his head in a beneficial posture. Say 'head down' combined with a little feel on the inside rein, then soften the rein to allow it, and the horse will soon comply.

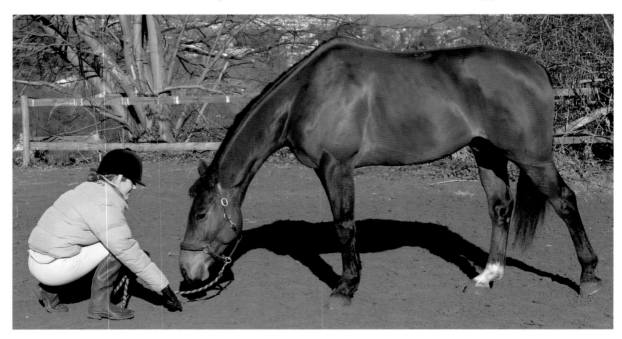

60 Teach your horse to open his mouth

It is very easy to teach a horse to open his mouth, but many owners struggle with it. Horses may clamp their teeth shut when you are trying to, for instance, bridle them, or check the conformation of the mouth and the suitability of a bit. It also helps if they will open up when you are squirting medicine in, and it also creates relaxation.

Open wide, please

One of the features of a tense, worried or frightened horse is that his jaws may be clamped shut. Working with a relaxed jaw and slightly open mouth is necessary for the horse to mouth his bit and accept it as an effective medium of communication (which he cannot do if his mouth is strapped shut), and to show that he is a willing partner, relaxed not tense. Administering medicine and other treatments is also easier if the horse is co-operative in this respect, and calm. Releasing the tension helps in many situations.

How do I teach this?

Stand by the horse's head, facing the front; then put your nearest hand under his jaw and over on to his face to steady his head, and put a finger in the corner of his mouth nearest you. There are no teeth here so you cannot be bitten.

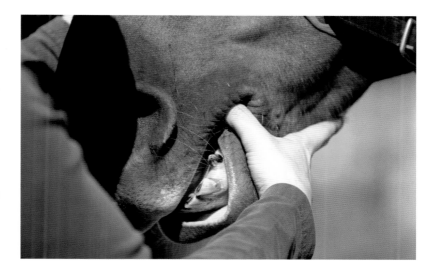

- Wiggle your finger on his tongue and say 'open', or whatever you wish, then praise him and give him a treat immediately, not several seconds later. Very few horses can resist the feeling of a finger in their mouth.
- In the course of my teaching I have often walked with a tense horse (having first made sure that the noseband is correctly adjusted loosely enough to allow the horse to open his mouth), and have gently put my finger in the corner of his mouth to loosen his jaw and relax him. I praise him and maybe give a mint.
- This action can be combined with the command 'open', as from the ground, and as with everything else that is well taught, the horse will soon associate the command with loosening his jaw, relaxing and opening his mouth a little.

61 How to manage a biter

It is often hard for people to accept that horses that bite usually do so in self-defence, attack being the best form of defence. Horses as a species are not generally aggressive, though many are made so by ill treatment. However, biting can be very intimidating – even a little nip from a horse can be painful, and many biters will do so indiscriminately.

How does it start?

Biting can be a male thing. Colts and stallions are certainly naturally prone to it in male company, and they may try it on with mares, though these will usually put them in their place. Although most male horses are gelded, if the biting habit is not controlled early on, it may continue after castration. Any horse, though, will learn to bite humans who treat them roughly. Bad handling and frustration are probably the prime causes of biting.

What can I do?

This is a situation that responds well to what the horse would perceive as self-punishment – if he bites and receives an unpleasant sensation but can't work out why, he may come to associate this behaviour with unpleasantness or even slight pain, and will think twice about it in the future, *but* without resenting humans.

I once trained at a yard with a very nippy stallion. Fortunately for me, on the way to his field was a convenient holly tree, so I would carefully break off a sprig and, on the way back, would hold it firmly in my free hand just in front of where his teeth usually landed. When his muzzle came round he got a very nasty prick from the holly, and he soon stopped biting me!

- Try sewing wire dog-grooming mitts to the sleeves of an old sweatshirt to wear when handling a biter: as he turns to bite, push your arm into his muzzle – but *without* looking at him or speaking.
- If you have a horse who lunges at you to bite as you approach him, squirt him in the face with a water pistol (see below).
- Remember that it's safest to tie up the biter short enough so that he cannot reach you when you are grooming, and handling him.
- Some people use a muzzle, and for horses that are genuinely savage, this may be necessary. However you handle a biter, the habit may be hard to break, but persevere!

62 How to manage a kicker

A horse can crack a brick wall and kill a human with one kick. Horses can kick backwards, sideways and forwards (cow kicking), and they can strike out with the forelegs. All are lethal weapons, sometimes defensive and sometimes aggressive ('kick them [a potentially hurtful human] before they kick/hurt you [the horse]'). So, if you want to keep a kicker, how do you deal with it?

Short-term tactics

Be familiar with the type of kicking your horse does mostly, keep your eyes open and your wits about you, and don't get into a position where he can kick you. Tie him up for attention so that he cannot swing his quarters into you and kick, and according to whether he strikes out in front, or kicks out behind, do not walk respectively directly in front of, or behind him.

Ask a helper to hold up the other leg on the same side as the one that he uses to kick out at you whilst you groom, because this will mean he has to keep it on the ground as he cannot balance with two legs on one side in the air. Be aware, though, that some horses will then try to half-rear when held or tied up.

Often, shouting at the horse will work followed by instant praise if he stops. Remember that most kickers have been abused and may not like being handled at all, so do not tease them. Do your work quickly, firmly and carefully, talking confidently to the horse and warning him vocally when he raises a leg – and always be on your guard, because horses can kick like lightning when they want to.

Long-term help

Confirmed kickers may not respond to any kind of retraining, but you could try using the glove-on-a-stick technique mentioned on page 85. Preferably have a sensible, confident person hold the horse, or tie him up. Stand away from the end that strikes or kicks, and gradually work towards it with the glove. When he threatens to kick say a firm 'no' and keep the glove where it is. When he stops, instantly remove the glove as his reward and praise him and give a treat. In this way, you should be able to progress a little further each time, ultimately using your hand instead of the glove.

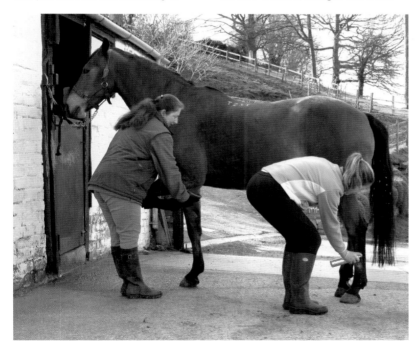

63 Teach your horse to lead safely

Nearly all domestic horses have to be led around. It is one of the earliest lessons foals should learn, and it often governs how a youngster will take to further education. Bad manners in hand when leading usually spread to other areas, because the horse does not feel the need to respect his handler. How do you change the habit of a lifetime?

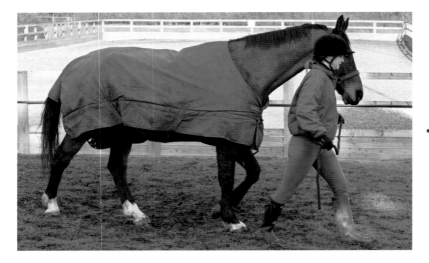

Leaders and followers

Correct leading should be modelled on how horses organize their natural pecking order – that is, with the leader/s leading and the others following in more or less single file. The operative word is 'following'.

It is often taught that we should walk at the horse's shoulder, but I disagree with this. Physically this can be dangerous, because if a horse shies at something on his other side his feet are level with yours and, strong boots notwithstanding, you can sustain quite an injury if he lands on your feet, and you could be knocked over.

He should accompany you so that his head is level with your body, or fractionally behind and to one side. This way he is showing respect by not getting in front of you, and you will not be trodden on if he does shy.

How do I teach this?

Teach the horse to understand the words 'no' and 'back'; you also might consider using a Tellington lead or a nose chain (see page 107).

- In his box, gently, use backward pressure-and-release with the headcollar/nose chain, and or prod his chest intermittently with your thumb or the head of a whip, or tap him

with the whip low down on his chest whilst asking him to back a step or two, saying 'back' at the same time. At the first sign of a backward step, stop the aid and praise him. Lead him forwards (saying 'walk on'), repeat and praise again.

- Take him outside, hold his leadrope short and lead him along level with his head. If he pulls or gets in front of you, say 'no' sternly, turn and back him a few steps using the above technique, then lead him forward again. Repeat this every time he comes ahead. Most horses learn to stay back in one session, but you must keep it up or they may revert.

Difficult horses

- With horses who swing round to face you in hand, stay facing them and push them backwards till they give in. If they fly around all over the place, firm (not rough), insistent handling with the chain or one of the more humane controller headcollars (see page 107) helps.
- With a really recalcitrant horse, use a *smooth* Spanish cavesson of leather-covered metal (available from suppliers of Iberian equipment) fitted midway between the nostrils and the bottom of the sharp cheekbones.
- Horses should always be accustomed to being handled and led equally from both sides, and must adapt their speed to yours, not vice versa. With difficult horses it may be necessary to have a handler on each side, one doing the training

and the other supporting and helping with control. The Tellington Team leading reins (see above), one with a chain end and one (the Zephyr lead) with a soft rope, can be used, one fitted on each side of the headcollar.

• To teach a horse to walk straight in hand, lead him along a fence on one side with you on the other, holding a long whip or twig so that whichever way he swings he is controlled. Use the whip behind your back to touch and tap (not hit) the stifle when the horse swings towards you, saying 'no' and praising him when he corrects himself.

Leading in public

• When leading on a public road, *always* place yourself between the horse and the traffic. The old way of leading from (in the UK and Ireland) the left side is really dangerous on our roads where traffic goes on the left, as horses can swing into it.

Some people even still lead on the right-hand side of the road heading into the flow of the traffic!

• Handlers should wear high visibility clothing and carry a whip in their right hand, just in case.

• If it is essential that you lead outside daylight hours, someone, preferably two people, should accompany the horses, carrying, ideally, motorists' lanterns showing white at the front and red at the back, and preferably with amber to the side.

64 Help a headshy horse

A horse who holds his head up high when you try to put the bridle on – even if for weeks or months or even years he has never had anything but sympathetic handling and riding – can be really maddening. We are always told that it is our fault or that of some other human, not the horse's, but it can still be infuriating. Why do horses do it, and what, if anything, can we do about it?

The bottom line

At the root of headshyness is always the horse's desire not to have his head handled because it has been uncomfortable or painful in the past, or because he knows that he is going to be tacked up and ridden, and he doesn't want that, either. Many horses throw up their heads when they see a bridle, but don't react to a headcollar.

What can I do?

- First get the vet to check whether or not the horse has an ear problem which is causing irritation or pain.
- Teach the horse to lower his head on request, being sure to reward him; increase gentle handling so that he gets used to the idea that there will not be any pain or discomfort.
- Start using gentle, but not tickly, massaging on the neck, also Shiatsu movements or Tellington Touches (see Further Reading). Gradually progress up to the ears, speaking confidently and praising the horse as long as he permits this. When he even thinks of resisting as your hand gets closer to his head, keep it there and continue touching. Do a little of this every time you visit the horse, and be sure to give lots of praise when he is compliant.
- Doing the same sort of thing as you graze the horse in hand can also help, provided you only do it in short spells and don't irritate him.
- The glove on a stick can help, but have someone hold the horse rather than tie him up, or you could create another problem: that of pulling back when tied.

Make sure that you are always really gentle when you handle the horse's head and put his bridle on, yet at the same time are confident and positive, remaining calm, expectant and in no rush, and you will make progress eventually. The important point is not to remove contact when he puts his head up, as this rewards his action and gets rid of the touching.

65 Teach your horse to travel safely

Transport problems constitute the largest single sector of behavioural problems in horses, and whole books and countless articles all over the world have been written about them. Most horses these days have to travel, if only to the vet occasionally, and a lorry or trailer journey can certainly be a fraught experience for horse and owner. What can we do to help?

Driver problems

Undoubtedly one of the main causes of horses disliking travelling and making a potentially dangerous fuss en route is because they are badly driven. Transport expert Dr Sharon E. Cregier of Canada sums it up very neatly by saying: 'Drive as though you had no brakes' – or you could imagine you have a glass of wine on the bonnet and must not spill a single drop.

The problem with the motion of the trailer or horsebox comes mainly during cornering, braking and accelerating, all of which have the potential to throw the horse off balance, and can really frighten him, creating bad memories for the future. Carry out these manoeuvres *extremely* slowly and carefully. Avoid potholes and, if possible, low tree branches scraping the vehicle.

Inside the vehicle

Make the inside of the lorry or trailer light in colour and airy, so it doesn't resemble a dark cave, and also make sure that the footing is secure, and that there is hay to eat. Some horses like a narrow partition, but others prefer it to be roomy: you will have to experiment to see what your horse prefers. Also, most horses like to be able see out, though there are some that don't. Remember that in many countries it is illegal to travel in the back of a trailer with your horse; however, it is all right to travel in the back of a horsebox.

It has been proved that most horses travel best tail to the engine, either directly front to back or in a herringbone fashion, head to the kerb. Horseboxes can be adapted for this, but most trailers cannot because of their balance. Also, many horses like to travel loose, and this is essential for a mare and foal.

For every hour travelled, the horse should have an hour's rest on arrival before starting work, plus an hour after work before the return journey.

Take a break

Travelling uses up as much energy in muscle use as working. It is advised that horses should not travel for more than two hours without a break, ideally unloading them and letting them graze and drink, to get the head down and assist the removal of debris and mucous from the lungs that can cause 'shipping fever'.

66 Teach your horse to load confidently

This is apparently the most common behaviour problem presented to clinicians at lecture-demonstrations held to discuss ways of improving 'problem horses'. Horses who are refusing to load can be seen at any equestrian event anywhere in the world, with any number of different ways of getting them to do so by persuasion and force. Here are a few tips, at least.

Why are some horses scared of loading?

Usually because they are unfamiliar with the vehicle (whether trailer or horsebox), because the ramp and inside are unwelcoming, because the ramp and floor make a strange and loud noise, because they do not reliably lead and go forward in hand, because people have forced them to load in the past, because they have had an accident, such as falling off the ramp, or because they associate it with a subsequent terrifying experience once the box gets under way.

How can I help ... ?

Again, any number of accounts and articles have been written on loading and travelling horses, and many man-hours spent at clinics seeking information and help. The following advice may be helpful:

- Making the vehicle familiar is always a good idea. Some people park their lorry or trailer in the horses' paddock with the ramp down (making sure that any sharp corners are guarded or padded). It can be left there for some time and horses may investigate it at will.
- Make the inside light coloured, put bedding on the ramp and floor, and hang haynets inside. Some people like to leave the exit ramp at the front open, if there is one, so that the horses can see and walk through, later closing it up to show them that it is not always open.
- A contributor to *Equine Behaviour,* the journal of The Equine Behaviour Forum, found that her horse would not enter vehicles with black ramps, even with bedding on,

but when she put red carpet on the ramp (!) her horse walked straight up. This prompted a dissertation later by a college student who found that black was a frightening colour, and that green was the least frightening colour for the ramp.

- Once a degree of familiarity has been achieved, buckets of feed may be placed nearer and nearer the vehicle, then on the ramp, then inside the vehicle near the back, and finally at the front, obviously to tempt horses in on their own.

And how do I start?

- When you make your first attempt at loading your horse, site the back of the vehicle to the sun, and ideally down a slight dip or slope so that the ramp is not discouragingly steep. Park it with one side against a hedge or fence, and lead the horse from his other side so as to minimize his escape routes.
- Make sure the horse is well trained, confident and co-operative in hand, and that he is familiar with the normal vocal commands.
- For the first few times it always helps to load up a horse's dam or friend first, feed them inside, then unload them. Remain confident, *expect* the horse to load and he often will, particularly if you have been through the above preliminaries. If he hesitates significantly, remain calm, place a hoof on the ramp and say 'walk on', praising and encouraging him.
- Lead the horse normally and *do not look at him*, which is almost certain to stop him.
- As soon as he is loaded, put up the breeching bar or chain; only then tie him up.
- Reward him with a feed and praise.
- To unload him: untie him first, then remove the breast bar or breeching bar/strap (in a trailer he will either unload forwards via a front ramp, or backwards via the back ramp), and lead him out or back him out – this must be done patiently, sometimes placing a hind foot on the ramp and allowing him to turn his head so that he can see where he is going. Quiet, still people on either side of the ramp can visually guide the horse down. When unloading forwards, the horse may go down rather quickly. Try to calm him by saying 'eeeeeasy' or whatever he understands, but be ready to go with him.

Horses with problems

The above technique can be used to retrain problem loaders, too, although some owners may well want professional help. However you decide to proceed, never let anyone thrash your horse to make him go into the box. It rarely works, and will surely make him a bad loader and traveller for life. It is important to be, as always, calm, firm and positive, and patient.

67 Teach your horse to lunge and long-rein

Both these techniques are age-old methods of training and exercising horses, but both, particularly lungeing, are often done badly. If, however, you start off the right way, you will find that both are invaluable for establishing the horse's response to the voice, and helping him to 'find his feet' without carrying the weight of the rider. You would be well advised to read what you can about both techniques; meanwhile the following advice may help.

Equipment

You will need the following items of equipment:
- a well-balanced lungeing whip that feels light in hand;
- a lungeing rein;
- ideally a leather lungeing cavesson with a padded metal noseband, as it is more comfortable than a headcollar, which may twist round, and it gives more control;
- most people use protective boots for all four legs, with over-reach boots in front;
- some people use a roller, with crupper and breastplate to keep it in place for attaching side-reins, although a saddle can be used;
- side reins, if used, should be adjusted so that the horse can extend his nose in front of the vertical, but still keep a contact with the bit. The use of side reins, however, can prevent horses going 'long and low', and…
- …will not encourage a correct preliminary posture: so these could wait till later.

Lungeing

- Your horse must comply with all the voice aids before beginning, and he must lead in hand well. Forget the whip to begin with, and instead have a helper walking on the outside of your horse with you on the inside; the lunge rein should be clipped to the front ring of the noseband and coiled in the hand furthest from your horse.
- Walk on a large (20m) circle, gradually working your way further away from your horse. He will try to follow you, so your helper now keeps him out on the circle. She should not speak – you are the trainer.
- A couple of circles on each rein of walking on, standing and walking on again are enough to start with. Gradually get the horse used to your standing in the middle with the helper on the outside.
- When the horse walks well and understands the routine, introduce a few steps of trot.
- As he gets the hang of this, introduce the whip: keep it still and purposeful. Pointed at the hip it has a driving effect, at the shoulder a slowing one, in front of the head a stopping effect. Your voice aids and your helper can back up the whip, until gradually the helper drops out.
- Your own body language is important: if you stand level with the horse's hip, it sends him forwards; stand level with his shoulder and it steadies him; and if you look him in the eye, square up and face his head, along with the voice and whip aids, he should stop.
- The main mistake most people make when lungeing is to work the horse on too small a circle, which is most damaging to the joints. Keep it at 20m in diameter. The second mistake is to trot the horse too fast, which is also damaging and encourages excitement. Steady trotting, encouraging 'head down', is what is wanted.
- Ten to 20 minutes is enough time on the lunge.
- Do not hesitate to recall your helper if you are having problems. They usually occur because the horse was not ready to progress to the next stage.

Long-reining

You will need another lungeing rein. Both are clipped to the side rings on the noseband, and pass either through the stirrups of the saddle (let down and tied under the girth to keep them still) or the lowest rings of the roller for a young or 'problem' horse. With a helper, get the horse used to the feel of the reins around his body and legs and over his back. You may find a buggy whip easier to handle for long-reining than a lungeing whip. There are different systems of long-reining, and you would be advised to read about these, so you can decide which system would suit you best.

- To begin with, use your helper to walk with the horse, initially in a large circle with you behind, holding the reins and talking encouragingly in terms the horse understands, especially 'walk on' and 'stand'.
- Generally horses understand long-reining quickly, and enjoy it. To turn right, say 'right', step to the horse's right and move both hands to the right, vice versa for the left. This 'pushes' the horse round with the outside rein in the classical manner whilst releasing the inside rein.
- To stop, say 'stand', slow your body movement and slightly tense your hands on the reins (don't pull) and/or turn your fingernails to the sky – another classical aid that works amazingly well on the ground or under saddle.

68 Loose school your horse

I have never come across a horse who did not enjoy loose schooling, done correctly. Anything the horse enjoys, which uses up his energy and stimulates, educates and exercises him, will improve his behaviour if done sensibly. Loose schooling certainly comes into that category, but many are afraid to try it.

What exactly is loose schooling?

The horse is taught by means of body language, voice aids, quiet whip aids and other means to work with no rider and not on a lungeing rein or in long reins – in other words, he is free, but within a safely fenced, enclosed space, normally a manège or indoor school.

Some skilled practitioners can work like this in a field with the horse wearing a roller or saddle and grass reins or side reins to stop him grazing although many would consider this unsafe in case the horse falls or gallops off and gets caught up.

In most methods the horse wears protective leg gear and a close-fitting headcollar. A horse who understands the usual voice commands (which he must before he is loose schooled) will soon pick up the idea, even if he has never been lunged or long-reined and so may not be fully familiar with the trainer's body language. He will almost certainly understand equine body language, though, and so will soon understand and follow the human version easily enough.

- Lead your horse into the enclosure, re-establish leading, walking, stopping and backing, then unclip your leadrope.
- A whip is not essential, but is useful to emphasize your movements. You can use a lungeing whip, a buggy whip or just a schooling whip (I find the Tellington white 'wand' – a white schooling whip – very useful as it is easily seen).
- Position yourself facing your horse's hip, then point the whip low down towards his hindquarters and say 'walk on', which he is almost certain to do.
- If he is doubtful, just touch him on the hindquarters with the whip and command again. As always, praise him for the smallest correct response. Correct him by saying 'no'.
- Use the following body language: a submissive, slouched body posture, head down and turned away, encourages him to slow down or come to you; a squared-up stance sends him away from you, or further to the outside of the school. To turn him, step towards his intended track and square yourself up in front of him, but not too aggressively – you don't want him to be afraid

of you, just to understand what you want. Use simple, familiar voice commands all the time. This is the same as you would use for lungeing.

You will find that most horses will imitate your actions. Prancing from you elicits prancing from them, crossing your legs and flexing in 'shoulder-in' will encourage shoulder-in from them. Believe it, it's true! Keep calm and focused on your horse, and practise thinking to him in pictures what you want him to do. Words of praise really involve and reward him; however, a pocketful of treats will get no work done because he will be thinking of them all the time and coming to you for them.

Loose jumping

I have known a few horses who jump free of their own free will when loose in a manège, but they are unusual. If yours doesn't, make a lane using jump blocks, stands and poles, if you have enough; alternatively, when the horse is experienced on the ground, you could ask several volunteers to stand about three metres away from the fence, quietly, arms down, to guide him round the outside of the school where you have set up, on the track, some simple, safe obstacles for him to hop over.

Of course, this can soon become a fine art, and it is tempting to jump the horse over fences that are too high.

However, there is nothing to be gained by this, and a lot to lose, unless the horse has a real talent for it. Even so, at first restrict it to about half a dozen jumps or so.

Send him along in walk first by leading him to the start of the lane which, at first, has only ground poles on it. Go alongside him outside the lane, commanding 'walk on'. Then gradually raise the poles, first to small cross-poles, and progress from there. Horses really are not stupid, and yours will soon get the idea of this new game, and may reach the point where he seeks out jumps if turned out in the manège, simply jumping for joy.

69 Use ground poles and an obstacle course

Any exercise that makes your horse think will really help improve his behaviour, balance his outlook, and teach him to think, look and consider where he is putting his feet – and most importantly, it will teach him to listen to you. Creating obstacle courses with poles, cones, buckets and straw bales is fun and educational.

What's the point of this?

Horses do not have an extended attention span, but they get bored easily with nothing to do. By nature, they do not sleep for many hours like dogs and cats. They are, actually, using their brains and making small but important decisions for about three-quarters of their 24 hours, seeking out different plants, remembering where they grow, foraging for roots, eating twigs and bark (perfectly normal) and also making probably twice daily trips to a water source. The horses have to remember where water is, and how to get there, and use their brains to plan and make the journey.

Compare this active-thought type of existence with that of the average domestic horse, especially if he is stabled. Giving him something to do can stimulate, entertain and educate him. Your only problem will be to think of enough new things.

Exactly what do I do?

- Gather together whatever safe equipment you have available – coloured and rustic poles, nail-free planks, logs, traffic cones, jump blocks or safe stands (no cups), upturned buckets, barrels, crates and so on.

- With the poles, set up a zig-zag corridor or a Tellington TEAM labyrinth to start with. Put a headcollar on your horse, and maybe a nose chain or TTEAM lead, and use their white 'wand'. It would be advisable to read what you can about the TTEAM system (see Further Reading) in order to give yourself ideas of different patterns and teaching devices.

- The idea is that you lead the horse through the labyrinth and get him to negotiate it and really think about

where he is going. He should go with his head lowered, looking where to place his feet, as you stoop a little and point the way ahead with the 'wand'. When he has been through twice, say once from each end, you can get him to walk over the poles, stopping when he is half way over, then walking on and perhaps backing over them when he is more confident.

- There are other TTEAM patterns for poles, such as the Star (poles radiating out from a central point with the ends at, say, 1m distances) and also the Pick-Up Sticks, which looks like a random jumble of poles 'dropped' on the ground, through which the horse has to pick his way. This is excellent practice for picking his way through woodland and stony places. You can also create your own patterns, of course.

- Ultimately it really does benefit horses' mental and physical agility to work through the patterns and cones. Depending on your horse and/or client, you can make the exercises as simple or advanced as you wish. Just do not get carried away in your enthusiasm and ask the horse for too much: they are nearly always willing to try.

- All the time, use familiar commands and lots of praise. Remember to use your mind to picture to the horse what you want.

- In the labyrinth, you can teach him to do a few steps of turn on the forehand and turn on the haunches to manoeuvre round the corners, then trot three steps on the straight parts, turn again, back down or completely through the labyrinth (quite advanced), and all sorts of other things. (To get a backing horse

to turn his quarters left, walk at his right shoulder and maybe hold out your left arm or the whip, and vice versa, commanding 'back' to help the horse to understand.)

- The use of the cones, buckets and other varied equipment is to create a route for him to walk or trot through, circling the objects, backing between them, crossing his legs sideways over poles, jumping little obstacles, and so on. If you do it with him he will catch on more quickly and actually enjoy it more.

- The ultimate achievement on the ground is for the horse to work free, with no leadrope at all, just you, your body language, your calm, positive attitude and his undivided, enthusiastic attention. This creates a real bond between you. Horses can learn a lot very quickly in the right circumstances.

105

70 Try using a nose chain

The use of a nose or stallion (US stud) chain is not common in the UK, even on stallions; however, it is fairly standard in the USA and some other countries, and not only for stallions. There is no doubt that you have much more control with a correctly used nose chain than with any ordinary headcollar, and even, in most cases, than with a snaffle bridle.

How does it work?

The idea of a chain over the nose may sound cruel to those not used to it and, like many pieces of equipment, it can be if misused. But because of the extra control it offers, I regard it as an item of safety equipment as well as training tack, particularly when leading a horse in open or public places. Note that a nose chain should *not* be used for tying up.

The nose bone is a sensitive part of the horse's anatomy, and the feel of a heavyweight, smooth chain here is sobering but not painful, provided the handler does not jab at it or exert a sustained pull. It elicits far more co-operation from a horse than the flat noseband of nylon or leather on an ordinary headcollar, and even than a snaffle bit. The chain is used tactfully and with small tugs in a pressure-and-release way, and when first fitted it should be gently pressed on the nose and released and slid gently from side to side to let the horse know that
here is something different, and worthy of respect.

Buy a heavyweight dog choker chain (with a ring at each end) for large breeds from a pet shop. Put the headcollar on the horse and thread the chain through the jaw ring and one side ring, twist it once round the noseband, thread it through the other side ring and back through the jaw ring again so both rings are through the jaw ring. You now clip your leadrope to the rings of the chain, *not* to the jaw ring.

The TTEAM lead (illustrated above) has a chain section that is fitted slightly differently: it is threaded through one side ring, twisted round the noseband, threaded through the

other side ring, passed up the side of the face and clipped to the upper ring on the side opposite to that from which you will be leading. You have to change it over when you wish to change sides.

71 Experiment with a controller headcollar or halter

There are various types and makes of 'controller' or 'restrainer' halter available, some less humane than others. They often work on the basis of tightening on the horse's head when he resists their pressure, the idea being that he learns that coming forwards gets rid of the pressure, but that pulling against it is very uncomfortable.

How do they work?

Most are made of fairly thin rope, sometimes in doubled lengths, made in such a way that when the leadrope, which fastens under the jaw, is pulled, or pulled on, the rope structure tightens around the horse's head. Designs vary, but most apply pressure to the poll and some to the nose.

They are meant to be used in a pressure-and-release way, not in a sustained pull normally (although I have seen some famous trainers use them in the latter way, stating that the horse was pulling against himself). Most are not intended for tying up horses.

They do certainly offer more control, when used correctly, than a plain headcollar, and can be useful for training horses who have learned to be difficult when led in hand, because a headcollar gives the handler very little control. They can also be used in situations where trouble is expected, such as exciting surroundings or when loading a badly behaved horse.

The type I dislike have strategically placed knots on the poll and/or behind the ears which intensify pressure. Some of these are said to work by activating acupressure points, but as a Shiatsu practitioner, I think this unlikely to happen in any reliable way.

If you wish to use such a headcollar or halter, I think it safest to have a thorough lesson from a handler who is trained in its use.

72 Stop a horse constantly nibbling at you

Nibbling at humans or other horses is a mainly natural but nevertheless annoying practice typical of young horses or foals that like to investigate everything and everyone. Teething youngsters may also do it. However, if it is not corrected straightaway it can develop into assertive or aggressive nipping as a way to demand attention or, more usually, titbits, and this more serious behaviour can easily become a habit.

Why does it start?

Nibbling is a foal's way of learning about the things, animals and humans in its brand new world. A horse's muzzle is the equivalent to our hands, so in fact this tendency is important in the foal's natural education. Young horses nibble when teething because their minds are constantly on their uncomfortable mouth, and chewing and nibbling anything or anyone within reach is the only way in which they can express their discomfort and try to relieve it.

Unfortunately, mature animals can also learn the practice of nipping and nibbling, usually to demand food treats when these are given often and indiscriminately. This is not good management or educational practice, and a nibble can very easily develop

into a hard nip or even a bite, as an expression of discontent or resentment for either the lack of titbits, or against anything or anyone else the horse does not like.

Read page 92, 'How to manage a biter', for dealing with mature horses. In younger ones (say, up to and including four or five years of age), correct them *firmly* when they nip at you with a stern '*no*', and maybe a raised hand to divert the muzzle. A poke on the muzzle with the end of your thumb as it comes towards you, a squirt with a water pistol, or contact with something unpleasant such as a wire brush, also often puts horses off nibbling and nipping, but these remedies have to be consistent until the habit has stopped or greatly lessened.

Shiatsu mouth work can help 'mouthy' horses, and you can do it yourself. There are many acupressure points around the muzzle: steadying the head with one hand, gently pinch all around the nostrils and lips and rub the chin and lips around with the flat of your hand. Also, with a wet hand, rub round back and forth inside the lips where they meet the gums with the web of your hand between thumb and index finger. Do this type of thing once or twice a day in addition to corrective training. Most horses find it relaxing and I have never known one to bite me when doing this.

73 Teach your horse to back safely

It is necessary for safety reasons to have a manoeuvrable horse both on the ground and under saddle. Well-mannered horses go forwards and back, and move over to either side on request or even automatically. It is particularly irritating to be faced with a horse who always plants himself in the doorway when you want to enter his stable.

What constitutes equine good manners?

What we regard as good manners, equines more probably consider to be submission! We want a horse who steps back without being asked when we enter his box. Most will move over easily enough when you say 'over', perhaps with a hand placed where a rider's leg would go (good pre-riding training for youngsters), but many do not like walking backwards and giving in to you.

Making a horse go back or move out of your way is definitely an act of dominance (watch horses in the field) but once learned, the habit shows respect and constitutes a part of what we term 'good manners'.

How should I teach my horse?

All you need is a headcollar, your own thumb and your voice. Stand in front and to one side of the horse, hold the leadrope short and, placing your flat hand on his chest, pull intermittently back on the rope, saying 'back'.

If this does not work, use the end of your thumb braced against your fist in a poking movement low down on the chest where there is a bone. Give a gentle but firm tug on the rope saying 'back', and follow it up immediately

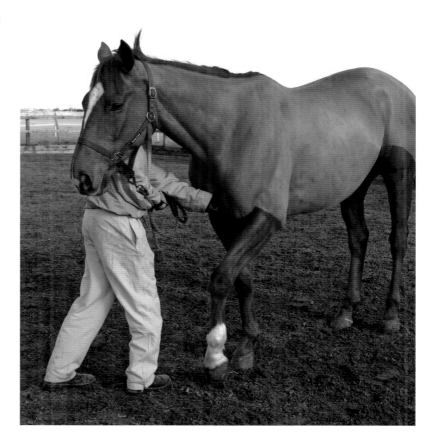

with a poke from your thumb. Usually you need do this only two, or at most three times, and the horse will move back. *Instantly* stop prodding and say 'good boy', and scratch his withers – but it has to be quick so that he understands.

Do this training routine a couple of times a day at first, and whenever

you enter his box say 'back' and, if necessary, poke him on the chest. Quite soon, all you should need is your voice, and eventually he will get to know that he is expected to step back when you enter his box. However, you must obtain this response every time, otherwise this submissive behaviour pattern will not become confirmed.

Under saddle

A change for the worse

Recently I wrote an article on the behaviour of ridden horses: it discussed whether horses were better behaved years ago, and it stimulated a very lively response from readers who, without exception, agreed that, yes, they *were* better behaved (by this I mean behaviour which is, or could become, unsafe for both horse and human in our society, for example shying, bucking, nervousness and a generally uncooperative attitude).

I also remember reading shortly afterwards a report from a leading UK equine charity, which said that most of the horses they took in had been sent to them because of behavioural problems, whereas only a decade earlier the main reasons had been, I believe, unsoundness or a change in the owners' circumstances.

A decade is not long for there to have been such a sea change in standards of equine behaviour. So what has gone wrong? The main reason is probably the closure of large numbers of high-standard livery stables and riding schools, with well-trained school horses; most of these businesses found that it was impossible to continue due to restrictive legislation and taxation, high levels of business rates, and the current 'compensation culture' that has spawned massive insurance premiums.

All this has led to a rash of do-it-yourself yards often operated by proprietors who have no background of high equestrian standards, and no depth of knowledge, who offer inadequate facilities, and who are often not even interested in horses. Their customers have no guiding hand, and often no knowledge themselves of how to really handle, ride and school horses, or to manage them so that they remain well, level-headed and co-operative. In a climate like this, it is no wonder that badly behaved horses are increasingly common.

Bad behaviour under saddle can be very frightening. It takes a courageous, cool-headed, competent rider even to stay on sometimes, let alone influence a horse's behaviour. There are few things more likely to break your nerve than to regularly ride, or come off, a horse whom you know is too much for you – and as far as the horse is concerned, this is often just due to a lack of schooling, correct management, work and discipline, all of which in the not-so-distant past were fundamental.

This section deals specifically with most of the problems people encounter, but it also covers techniques of prevention and the wider view of the principles of riding, training and re-training horses.

74 Ride with empathy

The word 'sympathetic' is often felt to have an outgoing sense of pity or tenderness towards a person or animal having problems. The word 'empathy' is a little different, in that it means being able to put yourself in someone else's place and to see things from their point of view. This may or may not involve pity and tenderness.

Ride instinctively

To ride with either sympathy or empathy takes a good deal of sensitivity on the part of the rider. Empathy in particular demands a high degree of being able to judge a horse's temperament, behaviour and intentions.

Horses in general are sensitive and observant, quick thinking and quick reacting, and they learn quickly, too. These are standard qualities of plains-dwelling prey animals, and are characteristics that have kept the species going for millions of years. They also need these qualities to enable them to live within their herd and to become an acceptable member of it to the other horses.

When it comes to working around horses, looking after them and riding them, these qualities need to be understood and respected by us. Although we are all born as innocents, life soon changes that, and we develop different acquired characteristics according to life's lessons. This means that not all horses come into the category of WYSIWYG (what you see is what you get), and despite the views of some behavioural therapists and trainers, some horses are what we would call crafty, scheming or devious because life (people) has (have) made them that way. Some will say that horses do not have the mental equipment to possess those qualities and to act on them, but I definitely disagree with that view, from close observation and experience.

Riding with consideration, tenderness, perhaps pity and a caring attitude is fine with a 'normal' horse or one who has had a bad time and become frightened, or is recovering from an illness or injury or poor condition – but empathy (which also includes caring) is more valuable, particularly when dealing with a horse who *seems* to be planning to get his own back on mankind through you. Such horses often feel that attack is the best form of defence.

Fair firmness and discipline, the expectation of good behaviour, and equestrian tact in applying these things does not mean being soft or weak. Weakness in people usually results in horses who are either insecure or domineering, depending on their temperament, although there are a few gems who will really look after novice and nervous riders, or those who don't know as much as the horse about what is going on.

How can I learn?

Being able to feel or tell what kind of horse is standing there in front of you (it's always a good idea to try to weigh up a horse thoroughly before you get on!) is a priceless ability – and it *can* be learned by opening your mind, using your head and your spirit, and riding and handling as many horses as you can. You will eventually realize that you can tell what a horse is thinking, what he is going to do, and also what he thinks of you.

Learning to understand horses'

'body language' or physical expressions and body attitudes is also important and a great help. Ultimately you will acquire almost an instinct for how a horse is feeling, where his real attention is, whether or not he is willing to learn or to do what you are asking, or whether he is genuinely feeling under the weather and should not work that day.

If you notice him look back casually at you without even moving his head, and at the same time, the hind leg on your side comes up ever so slightly, you could be forgiven for thinking that he is planning to kick you. If he looks at you with ears pricked, eyes wide and soft and points his muzzle towards your pocket, it's probably right to believe that he is enquiring about treats.

Riding with sympathy, or empathy, does not mean that you will be able to deal with every horse who comes your way, but it will enable you to get the best out of many different sorts – from angels to devils, the frightened, the know-alls, the laid back, the Cheating Charlies who wait till you're off your guard then have a go at you, and those who will pull out all the stops to do things with you.

You must learn when to be soft and giving, when to be firm and insistent, when to instil confidence, and when to get off. Learning to recognize when you are over-horsed is just as valuable as your other skills, and could save your life.

75 Cure napping

The word 'cure' is always a tricky one to use, but napping (also called jibbing, baulking or setting) is one of those behaviour problems that can often be successfully dealt with – and not all can. It can range from being a nuisance to actually dangerous, and manifests a determination in the horse to go no further, or even back.

Why do horses nap?

There are three main reasons:

1 The horse dislikes the activity you are asking of him.

2 The horse has never been taught to go forward and/or leave his herd.

3 The horse has insufficient confidence in/respect for his rider.

The first problem is reasonable and is the horse's only way of telling you that he hates or fears the activity. Before giving up, try making it as upbeat, non-stressful and enjoyable as you can with lots of praise.

The total absorption on the part of the horse of what I call 'the forward ethic' is crucial, and means that he will go forward whenever and wherever you ask, with or without other horses. The horse must regard you as his leader and protector when you are together, and you have to earn that regard. Then he will follow you (go forward for you) as he would a herd elder.

What can I do?

- Spend as much time as possible with your horse and see *yourself* as his leader. Attitude is everything! Remember: calm, firm and positive. Retrain leading in hand.

- Ride with another horse and gradually get further away from each other. Maybe split up on the homeward route and praise your horse for every forward step, but correct him with a confident 'no' when he naps. Leading out (in a nose chain for safety) helps many horses.

- If he naps at something frightening, let him examine it. If he spins round, apply firm aids to hold him facing in the right direction. Otherwise, spin him round in the opposite direction a few times, then stand him facing where you want to go and try again. If he runs back, strongly ask for forward movement or demand some steps of turn on the forehand to get control of the hindquarters.

- In dangerous situations such as in traffic, you may have to turn him a few times at *your* command so he thinks it is your idea, then go back the way you have come. Return with another horse at a quieter time.

76 Stop a bolter

The traditional view of a bolter is a horse who has lost control of his mind and is galloping in a blind panic. Most experienced horsemen agree that you cannot stop a horse in this state; an old-school horseman once said to me: '!f you ever think you have stopped a bolter, you haven't. You've stopped one that's just finished bolting.'

Why do horses bolt?

It is usually fear that sets off a real bolter, but great excitement can also do it, which then escalates to fear, particularly if the horse is in company and it all gets too much for him.

Short of bolting we have 'getting strong', 'running on', 'taking hold' and similar expressions. They all mean the same thing: the horse is galloping and not listening to his rider, *or* is doing what he has learned to do either as part of his job (such as racing) or because some previous rider has let him or made him do it, and he thinks it's permissible or what's wanted.

What can I do?

- First, if you know the horse is prone to this and you do not feel competent to control him, refuse to ride him. There are no Brownie points for heroics, only black marks and broken bones.
- If the horse is your own, have his teeth, mouth and bit, and his back and saddle checked in case pain is the cause.
- If it happens unexpectedly, much depends on where you are. Ideally, you should sit firm and deep, not too far forward, keep a straight line

from your elbow, through your hand to the horse's mouth (lowering the hands makes matters much worse) and spiral him down into increasingly smaller circles till he has nowhere to go. Then praise him for stopping a few seconds after he has actually stopped so he doesn't think he's being praised for galloping off.

- If you can't do this, exert an alternate strong feel-and-release on each rein to unsteady him, commanding 'stand' or 'walk on' (this has worked for me more than once).
- Another technique for a really 'strong' horse is to ram one rein over

the withers and hold it down hard, then do a strong pull-and-release action with the other rein. Change hands after a few tries. Always use the voice in a confident (!), commanding tone.

One mare I had who regularly did this was much more amenable if ridden in a bit she respected (no snaffle commanded respect – I used a pelham) and I had her flexed to the bit *before* I started to canter. A lot of horses who 'bolt' in a snaffle are fine if *sensitively ridden* in a curb, although the general feeling is *not* to change to a more severe bit.

77 Deal with a bucking horse

There are some bucks that nobody can sit to. Remember, even rodeo riders are only expected to stay on for, I think, eleven seconds. A bucking horse can be really frightening to many people, although some think it's fun – and funny.

Why do horses buck?

Horses usually buck because they are:

- in pain, usually in the back but maybe elsewhere;
- afraid the rider is going to cause them pain or distress;
- not confirmed in going forwards reliably;
- over-fed and under-exercised;
- have too little liberty and turnout, particularly play in company;
- are just feeling well and happy.

The bucks a horse makes because he is feeling good are not normally hard, vicious bucks, although they should not be allowed to get out of hand. The remedies for bucking for the other reasons are obvious.

Forget the old belief that horses cannot buck with their heads up or when they are going fast. One of the few who can, put me out of action for six months.

What can I do if it happens?

- In general 'sit up, get his head up and kick', in the words of an instructor I had many years ago.
- By all means, keep him moving forwards, and keep a reasonable feel on the rein, usually a fairly firm outside rein and a more variable but 'there' inside rein. If you feel the horse start to gather himself or change his gait in any way you have not asked for, growl loudly at him, give strong forward aids, maybe move up a gait and keep a contact. Keep him going in changing directions – turns, circles and serpentines – and keep a reasonable hold of his head. Too much contact can make matters worse, but too little just gives him a free hand.
- Spinning a horse round often stops a bucking spree before it starts, if you can feel it coming.

78 Deal with a rearing horse

Done in a controlled way during displays and performances, rearing is very impressive; at other times, however, it can be hair-raising because it is potentially so dangerous. It is a perfectly natural action for stallions, rigs and dominant geldings, but most other adult horses do not make a habit of rearing unless pushed to extremes.

Under what circumstances will horses rear?

Ridden horses rear from extreme excitement, provocation, fear, or if they are over-restrained when they want to move forward. A hard contact in these circumstances can certainly do it, but possibly the most common cause is pain or considerable discomfort in the mouth. Adjusting the bit too high in the mouth, and fastening the noseband too tightly come into this category, as does harsh use of the hands. Muddled aids and confusion are also a cause.

What should I do if it happens?

- Do *not* use the reins to keep yourself on, as this can bring the horse over backwards on top of you. Lean forwards with a loose contact and grab the mane, or put your arms round the horse's neck and *sit still.* Any movement can unbalance the horse and cause a horrific fall.
- If you have the presence of mind, tell him to walk on, and keep telling him till he does so, then praise him the instant he complies.
- Very competent and cool-headed riders may do various things to get the horse down, such as pulling his head down to one side, sliding off his back and then pulling him round, or bursting a plastic bag of water over his head as an unpleasant association. However, these actions are dangerous for most riders to attempt.
- As he comes down, straighten up, keep a gentle contact, and calmly tell him to trot forwards. Praise him and calm him as he does so. If he does not do so, turn him round and ask him to go in another direction. If you feel him preparing to go up again, circle him once (as he will find it difficult to rear if he is not straight), then ask him to trot on out of the circle.

All the possible causes should be investigated so that this dangerous behaviour does not become a habit.

79 Recognize when you need help

Most people will need help or advice at some point with their horses. As truly reliable 'on the spot' help and information seems less readily available due to today's livery situation, owners tend to ask each other what to do, and it is often hard for an owner in a quandary to decide whose advice to take.

Be honest with yourself

Probably the clearest indication of when you seriously need help with your horse, either from a professional or at least from a truly competent and understanding amateur, is when you start avoiding doing certain things or going along certain routes with your horse because you know he will play up, or will refuse to do what you ask, and you are afraid you may get hurt. If you are certain that what you are asking the horse is reasonable, if the problem is getting worse and the occasions when your horse is refusing to oblige are increasing, then you need help.

You also need help if you find that your nerve is going and you are becoming scared of riding – when you are finding any excuse not to ride today, or if you are asking someone else to ride your horse and feeling relieved when they do, and disappointed when they don't.

The problem may not be one of lack of confidence, but simply that you are not making progress (if you want to, that is) and do not know how to go on from your present level.

What should I do?

You may be able to find a good amateur rider who can help you on a regular basis, but usually the answer is to have lessons from a professional teacher. Finding one you like can be a minefield, however: one of the best ways to find someone suitable is by word of mouth; if you are in a particular equestrian organization, you could ask their local representative or head office, alternatively you could look out for advertisements in regional equestrian magazines, or check the cards placed in tack shops and in feed merchants.

Whoever you choose, give them a fair trial unless they appear to be harsh (as opposed to being firm and fair), and if you feel you aren't getting on, say so and try someone else.

80 Know ways to settle an excited horse

Excitement can be potentially dangerous if it escalates and the horse just stops listening to the rider, or starts behaving in a quite violent way. And even if that doesn't happen, an over-excited horse learns nothing in a schooling session, and doesn't perform well in competition; furthermore in certain situations he might work himself into a state of high excitement purely out of habit.

Why does my horse get so excited?

In many cases, over-excitement is caused because a horse is simply 'green' (meaning a novice), and has not had the experience to acquire that 'been there, done that' attitude so that nothing phases him. Many horses today live very restricted lives, and anything out of routine upsets or excites them.

Often the cause is feed that is too high in energy for the work the horse is doing, or for his temperament; for instance, only a very small amount of cereals will make some horses highly excitable.

If a horse has come to associate showgrounds, for instance, with exciting things going on, which they usually are, it may become a habit for him to become very excited, or if he knows he is going to some other exciting event, such as one that involves galloping and jumping, he will certainly get to know the routine, and may start trembling, sweating, playing up, or refusing to eat or co-operate.

How can I help?

The two main ways are to keep your horse on as low energy a diet as possible, and to get him out and about as much as you possibly can, giving him plenty of mental stimulation. Both these things will settle him in the medium to long term. Herbal calmers regularly in the feed and nutritional paste calmers for use only on the day help many horses.

In the shorter term it can be very difficult to settle such a horse. Riding with another familiar, quiet horse can help, or you could try walking or trotting around slowly in large circles (rising trot) on a moderate contact, whilst obviously speaking calmly to him. Correct him with 'no' when he plays up, and try to stay calm and firm yourself at all times.

81 Wake up a sluggish horse

Most people find riding a sluggish horse unrewarding and dispiriting. Only really nervous or unsteady riders like a horse who plods about slowly – but then, for them, such horses serve a valuable purpose. Otherwise, however, it can be frustrating, restrictive and even counterproductive to the average rider's ability and riding technique.

The causes of sluggishness

First of all, as with most problems, we have to consider that there may be a health reason for the horse's lack of energy.

- If the horse is fed an unbalanced, inadequate diet, this can certainly be one reason for sluggishness, so a nutritionist could be consulted.
- If he is sickening for something he could be listless, not merely sluggish, and an experienced horsemaster should be able to spot it and feel it; in this case you should certainly call the vet.
- If a horse is uncomfortable or in pain, again a vet may be needed for a thorough examination in order to diagnose the problem.
- Any problem with the teeth or mouth, tack, back, or feet and shoes can certainly create an understandable unwillingness to work enthusiastically.
- Ask yourself if the horse is sluggish all the time, or just when particular activities are asked for. If the latter, the reason is obvious: for some reason he just does not like that sort of work. Maybe he cannot cope with what is needed, and maybe he is just not suited to it.
- Maybe the horse has never been taught to go forward with energy and enthusiasm.
- Finally, your horse may have a very laid back temperament and will never be naturally energetic – though perhaps he could improve a little.

It's important to enlist knowledgeable and sympathetic help if you really do not know the reason for your horse's sluggishness; otherwise you could be working along entirely the wrong lines.

What can I do?

Assuming that any potential health problems have been investigated, as suggested above, we are left with dislike of the activity concerned, lack of schooling, or simply the horse's temperament. The same sort of answer is relevant to all those three reasons:

- You have to let the horse know that he is expected to move with a little more purpose in life, and you must make it light-hearted, fun and enjoyable for him: then it will be enjoyable for you.
- Adopt a cheerful 'yippee, this is great, let's go' attitude and *use your voice* in this way. Get on and, from his first step, talk to him in a very cheerful, upbeat way, using his name and 'walk on' or 'go on', whatever he understands. (I once reschooled a former circus horse using this technique and found that the only word he responded to was the French '*allez*', meaning 'go on'.)
- Give clear leg aids in a sideways tapping movement on his sides, lifting the legs out and tapping them both sideways (not backwards with the heels) on his sides, *and keep it up* till he speeds up. At the same time, keep on with the vocal encouragement, and *the instant* you get an improvement, stop the aid, say 'gooood boy' in a very approving tone, maybe stroke his neck or withers and see how much energy you get. Sit there and keep praising him, but stop all your other aids – accept it as a gift.
- The second he slows down, repeat the process, being sure to stop the aids as soon as you get a result, then praising him and going with it. Ceaseless nagging will make him worse.

What if that doesn't work?

Enlist the help of a sympathetic teacher to supervise, if necessary. If you have good control of your legs, you can wear blunt, rounded spurs, provided you don't kick hard with them. Just carrying a whip often helps: try just waving it up and down his side or hitting your own leg with it. Tapping behind your leg to reinforce the aid is the most you should need to do. All the time, remember the upbeat attitude and the instant praise.

Give him a break on a loose rein after, say, no more than five minutes, *provided* you have succeeded; then ask for just a few more minutes' effort, after which leave it for that day. The horse should soon get the idea of the extra effort required of him, and maintain it, provided you keep it enjoyable and praise him instantly so that he understands. Stopping the leg aid the moment he speeds up is crucial.

82 Manage a highly strung horse

Highly strung horses can shake the confidence of many riders, usually those who are not particularly brave (and there's nothing wrong with that) or those who have had one fall too many and feel that anything other than a patent safety ride (which doesn't have to be dull) is likely to ditch them again. What's the best way to cope?

Why do horses become highly strung?

There seem to be more highly strung horses nowadays than ever there were previously; almost certainly one reason for this is that horses do not get out and about like they used to, so they do not become 'worldly wise'. In many cases riders no longer hack out, often because the drivers on today's roads are so irresponsible.

Another reason could be that the riding methods now in common use are much harsher, a situation that does not encourage in the horse that important sense of trust and safety. Even that priceless gem, the genuine schoolmaster, can be ruined by bad riding.

The horse's natural temperament is a considerable factor in his propensity for nervousness, and this cannot always be attributed to what breed he is. Thoroughbreds, as an example, have never been bred for temperament and are regarded as naturally 'hot' – but they aren't all like that. Warmbloods are supposed to be bred specifically for their congenial nature – but again, they are certainly not all biddable, by any means.

Even with highly strung horses, management and upbringing, plus education of both horse and rider, can work wonders in ironing out problems.

Cultivating the right attitude

Owners of highly strung horses must first look to themselves, because horses, and particularly insecure and highly strung ones, always take their cue from their handlers and riders. Therefore your biggest challenge may be cultivating the calm, firm and positive attitude essential to all horsemen and women. Most horses need and want the guidance and protection of a leader-type person, and you may be able to establish this sort of rapport by singing a happy tune: this can have a remarkably calming effect on a horse. Very calming music as you school also helps – but not a constant bombardment of music in the stable area.

Maintaining a 'feet on the ground', laid-back attitude

yourself is most important: if the horse is highly strung and you are openly nervous, then you haven't much chance of being a calming influence. A habitually nervous rider and a nervous or highly strung horse are a bad combination. Being only slightly apprehensive is not so bad because you can still put on a convincing act of being confident: keep your head, your balance, your hand-holding feel on the reins and a loose seat and legs, and the horse will respond accordingly.

Most horses will pick up on what you are thinking, so it is important that you concentrate *not* on your emotions, but on what you want you and your horse to do together. Picture yourselves turning right with a good posture, correct bend and free, forward movement and you are very likely to get it. Also, be single minded in what you picture: so if your horse plays up a bit, think beyond it, picturing all the time what you want next, and not dwelling on what he has just done. Use your voice a lot in words he understands. Finally, get the horse out and about as much as you can, so that fewer things will cause him to get excited.

A management régime to keep him calm

- Turn out the highly strung horse as much as is reasonably possible with friends.
- Don't give him any cereals at all: some horses react badly to them.
- Try a herbal calmer in his feed.
- When he is in his stable, make sure he has a generous selection of different forages, fed from a low level or from on the ground.
- Give him clean straw bedding so that he can rootle about in it; this will keep him busy and calm for hours. Horses' minds in nature are almost constantly occupied seeking for food.
- Make him as comfortable as possible: peace and quiet if that's what he likes (study him closely), contact with a friendly horse next door, no more clothing than absolutely necessary, and as much contact with you as you can manage, leading him out and grazing him in hand, doing groundwork and different sorts of ridden exercise.

83 Make your horse good in company

Most horses naturally want to be together. Some horses, however, are not good with strange horses, and sometimes their owners actually put off taking their horses to places where there will be other horses, or when they do, they keep them away from others in a far corner. Is this the way to get them used to others, from afar, or is it just avoiding the issue?

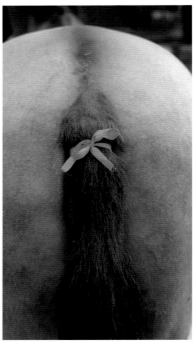

Teach the herd animals to be polite

In a herd situation, horses mix with familiar horses all the time; when strangers come along there will be squeals, stamps, threats and maybe actual contact with teeth and feet. All this is quite natural; however, when they are with humans it is an essential part of good manners that they restrict their interest to looking only, and certainly do not indulge in a free-for-all. If you let horses do no more than sniff each other, they will probably squeal and possibly strike out, which is unacceptable in public.

How can I influence the situation?

When you know you are going to meet strange horses and you are half expecting trouble, always have your horse in a nose chain (see page 106) or some kind of controller halter (see page 107) provided you know how to use it, if you are not riding him. (Remember that they are not for tying up or travelling in.) Alternatively, a firmly fitting but comfortable lungeing cavesson would be fine with your long leadrope or half-length lungeing rein clipped to the front ring.

With a helper if necessary, lead

or ride your horse at walk near the other horses, correcting him firmly if he plays up, and praising him when he is good. If you think he is likely to kick you must put a red ribbon on his tail, and if he is a youngster a green one; always try to stand him with his hind legs away from others. The more you expose your horse to others like this, the more he will get used to it and learn that he has to behave or he will be told off. It is largely a matter of your being in charge, and him knowing it.

84 Help your horse to deal with other animals

There is a widespread conviction in the horse world that horses are scared of pigs, and some are worried about any animal that is not equine. This is not natural, because in the wild other species of animal will be encountered all the time. In a domestic situation, however, it can be a real nuisance, and maybe dangerous, if the horse reacts violently.

Why might horses be afraid of other animals?

The reason is simply that they may not have had any experience of them. In the environment they were brought up in, there might have been only other horses with humans, dogs and cats, and your horse might never have had any experience of pigs, cows, sheep, ducks, hens or anything else on the stud he came from. Therefore to suddenly come across these when moved to his first home could be very traumatic for him.

Pigs in particular seem to cause problems for horses. Perhaps it is their slightly unnerving grunting, the squealing, the fact that their large ears flap about and partly obscure their small faces, and their strong smell.

How can I help?

As with most things of this nature, it is necessary to accustom your horse to seeing, and perhaps being with, other species as much as possible, ideally in the company of a horse who does not mind them, and humans who can control any untoward reactions.

Grazing the horse in a field next to, or even *with* other animals is useful if it can be arranged, or riding with the other horse, near and past them.

If you are riding near other animals and your horse tries to turn tail and bolt home, do your best to turn him back and at least just make him stand and look at them for as long as it takes for him to stop snorting and shaking. Try to take another accustomed horse with you. Talk to him confidently and conversationally – but don't say 'good boy' till he is. If he tries to move away, say 'no' and bring him back, then praise him.

Walk him past, when you can, flexed *away* from the 'foreign' animals, and praise him generously. Repeat the procedure within a few days, if possible, and he should improve.

85 Help your horse cope with unfamiliar surroundings

Horses are usually quite good about going to strange places, provided they are with people and maybe other horses they know and trust. However, it is not only young horses who lose their heads in new places: older horses suddenly confronted with a new place can react in just as lively a way as youngsters. What's the best way to help?

The advantage of 'away days'

Going to new and different places, and different types of place, should be a part of any horse's education. Today, many horses live very cloistered lives, often not even leaving their home yard for years. This may suit some horses and owners, but most people want to be able to get out and about, either hacking or boxing to other places for a ride or to attend a competitive event, an organized ride or some other occasion.

All this widens a horse's horizons and makes him worldly wise, even if he is not always calm and peaceful about it. Horses need mental stimulation, and going to different places and meeting other people and horses is an ideal way to do it. It also partly satisfies a horse's natural migratory nature: they are naturally curious, and usually enjoy experiencing new things, provided they are with other horses and people they trust.

How should I tackle it?

- Much depends on the horse. If he is young, naturally flighty, nervous, insecure or new to you, take a companion horse who has been everywhere and done everything, and behave as calmly and confidently as you can. They will sort things out between them, and the more expeditions you have together, the less of a hassle it will become.
- The first time I take a horse on a new route out hacking, I only walk because I don't want the horse to get the idea that we are always going to canter or go for a spin. The second time I trot, and the third time, depending on the surroundings, we'll have a canter.
- Take the horses along different routes, the other way around rides, and combine short routes if you can, so that the 'trainee' does not get in the habit of always doing certain things in certain places. It is also a good idea, if

hacking, once your horse has become fairly confident, to split up half way round a ride on the way home and on a route he is already used to.

- Another plan is to ride past your own gateway when coming home so that he does not develop the habit of automatically turning in, but listens to you instead.
- As he becomes familiar with different routes and places together with his friend, at some point you will have to take him there on his own. If you have a good relationship with your horse and he trusts you, you should be able to go it alone quite soon.
- Make sure your horse is well enough schooled to reliably answer your aids, otherwise he is not safe enough to ride out, anyway. If he will not leave the yard without his friend, treat it as napping (*see* page 114).
- Start by hacking in your locality, but using different routes from normal, and gradually widening your horizons. Even going the other way round a ride from normal seems different to a horse.
- If he spends a lot of time calling for other horses, he is not sufficiently confident in, or respectful of you, and feels insecure out of his normal surroundings, so you need to behave strongly and positively and work on *your* relationship as well.
- Whether you hack or go by trailer or horsebox to a new place, the principles are the same. Calm, firm and positive behaviour on your part are what is needed. By all means, box with a suitable friend to other places: it is usually more fun and it's good to have some help, not to mention your mobile 'phone, if there is any kind of problem or emergency. The more your horse sees of the world, the less it is likely to phase him.
- A good tip is to try to make a horse's first experience of a place pleasant. Go in good weather, and try to go at a time when it's fairly quiet; don't ask for anything exciting or difficult, and treat it all in a matter-of-fact sort of way.

Under saddle

86 Learn to cope with traffic

Traffic-shy horses are one of the biggest problems of modern life, and greatly restrict the riding lives of themselves and their owners. The fact that so many horses *are* good in traffic, and that it is perfectly possible to train, for example, police horses with a logical training programme, shows that initially it is our training that is at fault.

What do I need to consider before I start?

- The horse needs to be reliably responsive to all normal, ordinary aids. He must go forward and also stop without argument. He must learn 'stand', and be prepared to stand still for several minutes, if necessary, anywhere at all, as he may have to do this at cross-roads. It is also a good idea if he will move sideways and backwards when asked, not necessarily 'correctly', but so that he is co-operative and manoeuvrable, for safety's sake.

- If he wants to do a dropping he must keep moving, unnatural though this is, because if he stops without warning a vehicle could drive into his hind legs, with tragic consequences. Also, holding up traffic in this way will not endear you to all the other road users, and will add to the bad name already that is given to horses on the road by some riders.

- Normally, for significant work on roads, the horse will need shoeing. If he encounters gritty going or rough roads and feels uncomfortable, he will learn that roads are unpleasant and he may not then be so co-operative in general. For roads that are at all slippery, ask your farrier to fit road nails, as these are less disturbing to the hoof balance than studs. Many riders like to fit knee pads when riding on roads, too.

- Horse and rider must wear high visibility clothing, and if conditions are even slightly murky, a light showing white to the front, red to the back and ideally amber to the side, normally worn on the traffic-side stirrup. Cyclists' light belts are also good. I find that a tabard with 'L' plates on it is better than anything else for making drivers more considerate, as is carrying a long white stick or whip, perhaps with a tassel of fluorescent fabric on the end, or a 'high-viz' whip. These are easily visible to drivers, and seem to act like a blind person's white stick.

How do I start training?

A lot depends on your stable yard. The horse should be well used to being near traffic at home, with other horses or alone. Try to graze your horse in a field alongside a busy road where he will experience various vehicles such as fork-lift trucks, tractors, wagons, buses, screaming sirens, air brakes, buzzing trail bikes and so on. If this is not possible, try standing him in the gateway to the road with another traffic-safe horse, initially some way back, then moving gradually closer, praising him when he is quiet.

Start riding him in the field some distance from the fence, then gradually closer to it, in the company of the traffic-safe horse. When your horse accepts this calmly, ride him alone in the field and gradually, in the course of the following days or weeks, take him nearer and nearer to the traffic.

When the time comes at last to take the horses on the road, pick the quietest route you can, boxing there if necessary, and go with at least one other traffic-safe horse. Keep the other horse on the traffic side of your horse and slightly in front of him. Gauge your horse's reaction to everything, and gradually start riding behind the other horse, then now and again in front of him, and take the two further apart. Gradually introduce busier routes with the other horse, but try yours alone on the quiet ones, perhaps with someone following on foot or on a bike in case of problems.

If you encounter a problem, from a training point of view it is best to face up to it and stand still if you possibly can before continuing; however, from a safety viewpoint it may be safer to turn the horse round once or twice and then go back the way you have come, or turn along another route, returning with your companion on another, quieter occasion.

This gradual acclimatizing is the proven way of getting horses used to anything. However, it is important that you are confident yourself, or the horse will pick up on your nerves and you may actually turn him *into* a horse who will always be afraid of traffic.

129

87 How to keep your horse interested in schooling

Schooling can, to a horse, be boring, distressing and even painful, or it can be interesting, enjoyable and leave him with a feeling of achievement, so far as we can tell. Memories of previously fulfilling sessions make horses keen to work and learn more, whereas boredom, anxiety, tension and pain sicken horses more quickly than anything else.

What is the point of schooling?

The whole purpose of schooling is to make a horse a pleasant, reliable and safe ride and to teach him to do the kind of work you have in mind for him. Inherent in these aims is the need to build up the horse's muscles correctly so that he acquires the physical strength and suppleness to perform as you require of him under saddle, within his capabilities.

Make a plan of action to create and maintain interest

A manege is not essential for schooling although one with a well-drained, springy surface, neither too hard nor deep, is a definite advantage. A lot of good work can be done in a decent field, or out hacking in suitable areas and this certainly keeps horses fresh.

If schooling while out hacking, don't school constantly. Give the horse frequent breaks – spells looking around, striding out on a long rein or having fun, maybe popping over little obstacles or negotiating hazards. If schooling in a manege or similar area, keep your session to about 30 minutes. Remember the old rule to finish on a good note. If the horse has achieved what you wanted in 20 minutes, praise and stop. Always finish with something

he enjoys and does well, and praise him instantly. Keep your attitude upbeat and positive. Horses read our minds and know what mood we're in – and it's catching.

It is important both to have a flexible plan of what you want to work on before you start, and also not to spend more than a few minutes per session on one particular task.

REMEMBER THE 4 Ps

- Position the horse so that he can actually achieve your request.
- Let him Perform the movement, *without* constantly applying the aid.
- Instantly Praise him for achievement otherwise he doesn't know whether he has done right, has no reward and no reason to co-operate in future.
- RePeat once, and once only.

Before you begin work, warm up on as long a rein as you dare, considering safety and control if the horse is spooky (ideally a loose, free rein) so that the horse can limber up and stride out at walk, trot and canter in an uninhibited way.

Increase the difficulty of the work in tiny increments to give the horse a positive feeling. Study good books on schooling and work in a logical progression. Over-taxing a horse mentally or physically is a sure way to sour him.

Make it an ambition not to do more than one full circuit of the school at a time. There is nothing more soul-destroying for the horse than to slog around and around and around the track. Physically this can encourage horses to psychologically 'lean' on the fence and ignore the rider's outside aids and/or can stop the rider using the outside aids because she doesn't feel the need. Intelligent, willing horses may become frantic with boredom and the more phlegmatic type switch off. Ride different shapes such as circles, demi-voltes, loops, serpentines, squares and diamonds, figures-of-eight comprising two circles but also two triangles, the apex of each meeting at X, and change the rein in different ways, not only across the diagonal. Invent your own patterns.

In order to maintain the health and optimum function (including development) of muscle tissue the horse *must* be allowed to stretch freely between *short* work sessions. Tissues must be loose and relaxed for blood, lymph and energy to flow through them. Muscles work by contracting which 'tightens up' the tissues.

Sustained contraction or a forced outline can cause oxygen deprivation, toxin accumulation, tissue damage, strain and pain – all bound to make horses resent schooling.

Never work a horse, therefore, for more than a very few minutes (up to five for a fit, schooled horse, much less for a green one) without a buckle-end break (walking or just standing), on a completely loose rein. Make sure your reins are long enough to allow this.

Under saddle

88 Help a horse who hates jumping

We must all have witnessed horses being forced to jump when clearly they don't want to – sometimes even under the orders of an instructor. It isn't true that you can't force a horse to jump; I have known many who evidently didn't dare *not* jump, which is an appalling indictment on the attitude of their riders and trainers.

Why does this happen?

There are several reasons why a horse might not want to jump:
- Pain = past, present, expected = from spurs, whip, bit/hands, ill-fitting saddle, rider banging on the back, poles hitting the legs, and injuries or weakness causing pain during effort.
- Restrictive riding (loading him up with restrictive tack); not giving the horse his head on the approach, so preventing him from seeing the obstacle clearly; holding him back too much so that he cannot make enough of an effort; preventing him stretching over the obstacle; and

jabbing his head up too soon before landing.
- Continually spurring and whipping the horse or pony when he is doing his best already.
- Over-facing the horse with obstacles he knows he cannot cope with, or through jumping too often and demanding maximum physical effort.
- The horse knowing that the rider is frightened.
- Being made to jump when he is unwell, tired or injured.

What can I do?

Decide to give the horse a year off from jumping, and get him checked by

a vet and fully treated for any physical problems. During this break, give the horse a holiday, then try other pursuits not involving jumping. Make sure he is not in any pain or discomfort, that he is ridden sympathetically, and that he enjoys life.

Then, start from scratch from poles on the ground under a skilled and caring teacher, and see how far you get. Often a season's drag-hunting at this point works well. If the horse still hates jumping after this, don't ask him to do it. If you really want a jumper, sell or loan him to a good home for flatwork only. If you have a job you hate, you can always look for another one. The horse can't.

132

89 Cure fear of ditches or water

Fear of water can range from anything from refusing to cross water running across a road, to refusal to enter a river, lake or the sea, and particularly, refusing to jump into water. Many horses never have to tackle water in their lives, but if it is not addressed in the course of a horse's education, then it may cause problems at unexpected times in the future.

Why are some horses frightened of water?

There is a theory that horses with desert ancestors have an instinctive fear of water. However, one good reason could be that horses are normally extremely careful where they put their feet because as prey animals, their feet and legs are their means of flight, and therefore their security. Water usually obscures what is underneath it, particularly in the daylight if the surface glitters.

How can I reassure my horse that water is safe?

- First of all, make sure that it is. If ever you take your horse into water and he has a bad experience, he may never go in again – although some are very forgiving.
- As with any learning process, start easily and slowly. I once stood in a stream for an hour (no rubber boots in those days) coaxing my youngster in. He never did set foot in it, but finally leapt from one bank to the other.
- The horse must first be obedient to normal requests such as 'walk on' and 'over' (to get him to move sideways). At home, set a hosepipe running across the yard (though make sure that it is not snaking about or gushing water). Maybe with patient, knowledgeable help, ask him to at first walk round it and at the edge, then into the edge with lots of praise and mints, and finally through it. Make a big fuss of him when successful, then stop. Try again till he does this quite willingly.
- Use the same technique with shallow puddles, then deeper ones, little flows across tracks, streams, fords (particularly useful if shallow), and progress from there. As ever, an experienced schoolmaster horse will be invaluable to give yours a lead. One day, he may be able to return the favour. Never let him turn away.

90 Cope with shying

When a horse shies it usually happens without warning: this is because it is his natural reaction, as a quick-thinking prey animal, to something startling or frightening which he suddenly sees or hears near him, and which causes him to leap sideways without thinking where he is leaping to. It can be equally frightening to the rider.

How else does the horse react?

The horse doesn't always jump away sideways when he shies; he is just as likely to spin round or leap directly away from whatever the monster is – so if it is by his left hip he may jump forwards and right, for instance.

Shying can almost immediately develop into napping, or worse running backwards or rearing, the latter being particularly dangerous. Sometimes after shying the horse might set off in a headlong gallop. All these behaviours are potentially hazardous, so it is important to cope with the shy before it develops into anything else.

What can I do?

The horse is most likely to jump away sideways, but he will quickly turn his head *towards* the object and his hindquarters away from it. If you know your horse well you may be able to anticipate what will happen, and have an almost instinctive idea of what to do, and you can act a split second or more before he does. He may even give you a few seconds warning by hanging back, prancing a little with his ears hard forward, or staring towards the problem.

- To keep control you should bend him away from whatever he is shying at. Let's imagine that the problem is to his left. He has shied to the right, but his head will be looking left and his quarters swinging right. Immediately and firmly turn his head to the right with strong, *sideways* pressure on his neck with the left rein and pulsing pulls on the right rein. Your right leg should act behind the girth to push

the hindquarters over to the left.

- Ideally, once you have established control, you should turn the horse in this flexion to the right and let him look at whatever caused the shy; however, this depends on the surrounding conditions, and it may not be possible, say, in traffic.

- Even so, if you can, face him at the problem, ask him to stand and talk confidently to him. *Do not say 'good boy' unless he stands still*. If he jigs about, say 'no' and a long drawn-out 'all right' and 'easy'. Praise him the instant he does stand still.

- Stroke his neck firmly and hold him gently but reassuringly with your legs. It also often helps to 'hug' the horse's neck with the reins and hands, keeping them close to the neck sideways.

- What will *not* help the situation is tenseness on your part, even though

it is inevitably difficult to relax. But try your best, and if he shies again or tries to move away, then use the same techniques.

- If the circumstances are such that you can't do all this, flex him away from the object and shoulder-in/leg yield past it (in right flexion in this case). Flexing the horse away from the problem gives you control, and seems to give him more confidence, perhaps because he feels that *you* are in command of the situation and are moving things on, although he can still see it out of his left eye.

How can I stop him shying in future?

Shying is a natural reaction, and the best-mannered horses will do it if they are sufficiently startled.

To lessen its occurrence, you should concentrate on your schooling work and voice aids (particularly 'stand', 'head down' and 'walk on') so that your horse listens to and trusts you more and more, and obedience becomes a habit. Make him very manoeuvrable, with transitions, lateral work and turns on the forehand and haunches, so that he almost automatically responds to your correcting aids. A good exercise is to have regular, short sessions in which you practise placing every step, maybe over obstacles, mentally and physically, so that your horse knows that, basically, you, and not he, are directing operations.

If your horse feels confident with you, and knows that you will not take him into any risky situation, he will feel much less inclined to shy, but compliance with your aids should become 'programmed' in.

135

91 Teach your horse not to fidget

Some people don't mind if their horse fidgets either on the ground or under saddle. Many more, though, find it somewhat irritating to have a horse constantly fidgeting on the ground, or refusing to stand at a crossroads, or when you stop out hacking to talk to someone. We regard it as bad manners, but horses have to be taught this.

Why do horses fidget?

Many horses find it difficult to stand still and do nothing whilst other, more exciting things are going on, because they are naturally active animals and normally are only still when resting. When ridden they are not resting naturally even at halt, so they may be expected to move unless they are taught otherwise. Young and highly strung horses fidget about, but so do older ones who have never been taught manners.

Proper standards of manners are that horses should stand to attention at the back of their box, or should stand still and wait whether mounted, tied up, held or loose – a very useful and safe habit for them to get into.

What can I do?

- First, make sure that your horse is not made over-energetic by a diet which is too high in energy, also that he is comfortable, and that he has enough work and liberty to keep him level-headed.
- Under saddle, make a habit of stopping and standing still anywhere, using the familiar 'stand' word and whatever physical aids you use to stop. Stroke the horse's neck and praise him, and just sit there for a few seconds, then praise him again, and continue in walk.
- If he moves before you want him to, say 'no' instantly, place him exactly where he was, say 'stand', stroke and praise him, and just sit there. Either talk to someone or fiddle with your clothes or his tack. Be happy with several seconds at first, then walk on. Gradually he should stand still and wait whilst you have a conversation or wait for traffic to clear, before you go on your way.

A very few consistent sessions of this sort of practice will produce a great improvement, and you should keep it up by expecting and implementing it all the time as a matter of habit.

92 Keep your horse listening to you

It is normal for a horse to look around him anywhere. At risk of boring readers by saying it again, he is a prey animal, and needs to check out his environment for danger or anything new and suspicious. However, when people are present his attention should be mostly on them, and this should certainly take precedence when he is under saddle.

Disadvantages of lack of attention

Put simply, a horse who is not listening to his rider most of the time is not under reasonable control, and this could be potentially dangerous. If his attention is firmly on something else, anything you try to do to counteract any unwanted behaviour may not, as a result, have any effect, the horse will operate on his own agenda, control and co-operation may be completely forgotten, and injuries could result.

Horses are good at multi-tasking, which is an excellent survival strategy, but for safety there needs to be a main focus of attention – and that focus is *you*.

What can I do?

- Make sure that the horse not only knows his name, but responds to it fairly promptly. Use it a lot – whenever you visit him or call him in from the field, before you enter his box and before you ask him to do something specific.
- When standing with him on the ground and his attention is elsewhere, give little tugs on the leadrope or on the rein nearest you if he is bridled, say his name, and keep saying it till he turns away from

whatever it was and looks at you. Praise him. Then relax and wait for his attention to wander again, as it will, allow him a few seconds, then repeat and praise. Now extend this to ridden work.

- Under saddle, whether standing or moving, he may look around to some extent when warming up and, of course, when hacking. Once warmed up in the manège, say his name and get his attention, with

either a tap of your inside leg or a feel on your inside rein, until he listens to you (one or both ears will flick back towards you), praising him instantly when he does.

- Out hacking, part of the benefit of hacking is to let him see different things, and this is fine *provided* that the instant you ask for his attention you get it. Inattentive horses are not under control.

93 Cure your horse's dislike of being girthed up

There are many horses who do not like being girthed up and, having watched many people do it, I am not surprised. It must be a most uncomfortable procedure, and possibly painful if skin is pinched under the girth. Also, of course, the girth is round the ribcage and must, to some extent, interfere with the horse's breathing.

On carrying a saddle (the horse, that is)

A riding horse should be able to carry a saddle naturally. Looking at a horse from the side, you should be able to draw a line straight upwards from the point of the elbow, and it should come in front of the withers. When the saddle is girthed up, this conformation will ensure that the girth lies well back from the elbow, so will not interfere with it. A few inches behind the elbow there should be a natural girth groove. Such a horse will carry a saddle naturally and comfortably, and his girth will lie back from the elbows; it won't need to be very tight for normal riding.

You should just be able to slide the flat of your fingers under the front part of the girth when the horse is mounted. Loose girths could possibly cause rubbing, but I have seen several skilful riders ride in demonstrations or for fun without a girth.

How can I help?

- For comfort, consider a girth that is shaped back away from the elbow, certainly if the horse does not have a helpful conformation, and also one that has elastic inserts at both ends or in the middle so that there is an even pull, not a lopsided one, on the saddle when the horse breathes and moves.
- The best way to girth up is to have

a girth which is long enough to initially buckle on the first holes of both sets of girth straps without having to be pulled tight, even if the horse 'blows out', so causing no discomfort. Tighten it one hole at a time on alternate sides, taking a few minutes whilst you put on other tack in between.

- After reaching the final holes before

mounting, carefully pull the horse's forelegs forwards and out (not up), holding the knee *and* the fetlock, for support. This smoothes out the skin under the girth.

- Praise and reward the horse for good behaviour during girthing, and you should see some improvement; however, horses often remain wary of the process.

94 Teach your horse to lead file or hack alone

Horses who won't hack out alone place a significant restriction on their usefulness. It is also good to have a horse who will lead file to set an example to others such as youngsters or nervous horses. Some horses who have a naturally fast gait but who will not go first will hold back from those in front, and this can actually spoil their paces.

What is the problem here?

Basically, these two related behaviours are caused by a lack of confidence of the horse in the rider. When under saddle, the horse needs to know that the rider is trustworthy, and to trust her enough to go *anywhere* she takes them both: obviously this places a great onus of responsibility on the rider. Genuine schoolmaster horses who look after their riders will do this anyway, and some horses are just so confident, sensible and probably previously well trained that they do it without thinking.

Horses who have previously had a bad experience out hacking may refuse to lead file or to go alone, notwithstanding a confident rider and preferring to rely on the company and judgement of other horses.

What can I do?

- Initially it is essential to work on your 'bond' or relationship. Such horses need a leader/protector-type owner whom they trust, and this cannot be developed in a few days or even weeks.
- Try to find at least one other confident and sensible horse, ideally with similar gaits to yours, to hack with. Keep yours on the inside at first, then behind, and gradually try overtaking each other, then getting further and further apart, splitting up on the way home if possible, taking different bridleways or quiet routes,

and meeting up again part way round. This sort of routine will help a great deal in time.
- You need to be very calm, firm and positive – again – for the horse to feel safe with you. Do not initially take him on routes where you know there are frightening things – keep it

straightforward and be strong in your resolve.
- Someone walking with you or on a bike can also help.
- Always remember that praise and fuss when the horse behaves, plus relaxation on your part, will help him a great deal.

95 Help a horse to go straight

General l'Hotte, the French classical master, laid down three principles of schooling: Calm, Forward and Straight. These three words are emblazoned inside the foreheads of many good riders because they are so important. 'Straight' is not natural to many horses, and is made worse by a rider who, herself, is not straight and doesn't know it!

What does straightness mean exactly?

The most basic definition of 'straight' when applied to horses is that the hind feet follow exactly in the tracks of the forefeet, and the four legs all move in the same forwards-backwards plane. This applies whether the horse is on a straight line or on a bend or circle (a bend being a small part of a circle).

The old masters of classical equitation set down what they believed to be correct standards for equine movement and posture based on the horse's natural physique and movement, and these standards remain our criteria today, although some are clearly ignored (such as the modern practice of making horses go with the front line of their faces behind the vertical, with the chin held towards the chest).

One of the most ancient of the modern classical breeds, the Pura Espagñol (Pure Spanish or Andalusian), has actually been bred to dish or throw the forelegs outwards in an arc as this is felt to be showy for display purposes; but the forefeet still have to land 'straight' and the hind feet to land on the same line.

Why is straightness important?

Straightness is important because it indicates that the horse is accepting and obeying the rider's aids and

going 'true', with a thrust of energy directly from hindquarters to forehand along the horse's spine. This creates economy of energy, and correct, even muscle development, making for better and easier work in future. It is also felt that 'true' gaits are more beautiful for us to watch.

How do I know whether my horse is straight?

The easiest way is to walk him along undisturbed ground such as a fresh foreshore when the tide has gone out, or a freshly harrowed manège or bare soil area. Sit quite still and relaxed on a loose rein without influencing the horse to be straight, look directly at a particular marker, say A from C or a tree, then check the line of hoofprints he has made. He may wiggle about, but his hind prints should follow his fore prints, and not be to one side of them.

And what about me?

It is often hard to know whether or not you are sitting straight and evenly in the saddle. The best way to check yourself, until you get the feel of sitting straight, is to get a knowledgeable friend or teacher to watch you from behind and then tell you the truth. Adjust your seat (if necessary) till she tells you that you are straight, and work at getting the feel of it. Make sure your saddle is on straight, too.

How can I improve our straightness?

Once you have the feel of straightness, an excellent way to improve it is to get into the habit of riding within 'the corridor of the aids', a valuable classical concept. Imagine, whether you are on a straight line or a curve, that you are riding along a narrow corridor, the walls formed by the reins and your legs, and the horse has to remain within those

walls. When he deviates he hits the wall -- your rein and leg on that side; pressure from them straightens him up, plus a tweak on the opposite rein.

Also, get into the habit of looking directly ahead to where you are going when on a straight line, not down at your horse, and feeling whether or not the horse's hindquarters are directly underneath your seat bones (the lowest part of your pelvis) or held out to one side. You cannot do this if your seat

muscles are tense and, therefore, hard, so relax and make them and your thigh muscles really soft and loose.

On a circle or bend, the horse's hind feet must also follow the fore feet unless the rider deliberately asks otherwise (such as in shoulder- or quarters-out or in on a bend). Once you can feel straightness under you on a straight line you will soon learn to feel it, or lack of it, on a curve and can apply your seat and leg aids accordingly.

96 Teach your horse to move backwards and sideways

Many people have never tried to get their horses to move backwards and sideways when ridden. However, this sort of basic manoeuvrability is essential for safety, and all horses should learn to go forwards, sideways and backwards (though not upwards or downwards!).

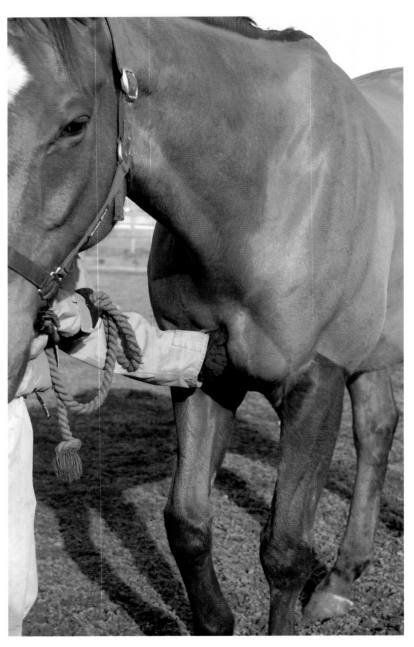

Aren't these quite advanced movements?

Some people would have you believe so, and maybe they are if you are aiming to do them strictly correctly. As a child, I was taught by a classically orientated teacher, on ponies he trained beautifully on long reins, to do good, correct rein-backs, half passes and full passes (rarely heard of these days outside the classical milieu), and clearly remember doing them from quite an early age on very ordinary riding-school ponies, with no hassle.

A horse who is amenable, co-operative and easy to ride is also manoeuvrable: in other words, you can put him anywhere you need to quite easily. It is not advanced – it is important for safety.

Teaching your horse to move backwards

In the stable, stand your horse towards the front of the box so he has room to move backwards. Stand at his head to one side, lightly pressing the flat of your hand on his chest, say 'back' and walk one step towards him, imagining to him that he moves backwards. Look over his tail to where you want him to move. Praise him, and stop the aid the instant he complies.

It may be necessary to increase the pressure of your hand, but he should move back from this. If he does not, make a fist and brace your thumb against the side of your index finger so that its end protrudes, and prod him in an on-and-off pressure low down on the chest, saying 'back', walking towards him and increasing the pressure of the prods, if necessary. I have never known this to fail.

In the manège, do this from the ground, then mount and ask for it from the saddle. Do *not* haul backwards on the reins: this will not work and is appalling riding. Just keep giving gentle feels on the reins and say 'back' to ask for rein-back. Lighten your seat a little by taking more weight down the insides of your thighs, and lean forwards *very* slightly (but do not actually come out of the saddle). Squeeze and brush backwards with your legs and say 'back' (*see* photo, top right). It would help to have a friend apply the familiar pressure on the chest from hand or thumb. Practise this once or twice only, every day, till he can do it foot-perfectly.

How to get your horse to move sideways

Start in the stable. Place the flat of your hand about where your leg would go if mounted, press firmly on and off, and say either 'sideways' or 'over', looking over his back to where you want him to go and imagining him moving over (*see* photo, bottom right). If he doesn't understand, get a friend to push, again on and off, on his thigh while you push his head gently away with your other hand. He will catch on to this very soon. As always, praise profusely the instant he moves a fraction in the right direction.

To transfer his new knowledge to ridden work, have your friend to hand, if possible. Bring the horse to a relaxed halt and stroke him. Aim to move him to the right: to do this, simultaneously press sideways with your left rein and leg, put your weight lightly into your right seatbone (horses follow your weight), move your right hand to

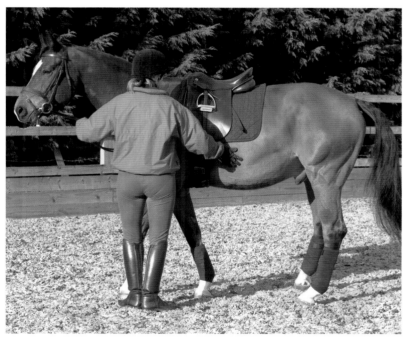

the right (not downwards – keep your elbow bent) and say whatever word you have chosen, picturing him moving right and looking there. The friend can supplement, if required, as in the stable.

A simplified version of this is to move both hands to the right, put your weight on to the right seatbone, and

use your left leg back from the hip, plus as always the voice. The instant you get even the slightest movement in the correct direction, stop the aid and praise him profusely with your voice, and repeat the exercise once. Don't keep doing it then, but do it regularly in both directions whenever you ride.

97 Teach your horse to deal with gates sensibly

It is really useful if your horse is co-operative when you have to open and shut a gate – or will even open them for you, provided you can find one that opens easily from the saddle. A horse of mine used to push the gate open with his nose, turn about the forehand round the end of the gate, and push it closed again. All I had to do was operate the catch and sit there. Magic!

There are gates and gates ...

If you are hacking out along bridleways, you are almost sure, sooner or later, to encounter a gate which has to be opened and closed. Many gates are difficult to open from the saddle so you have to get off and on again, so

we'll deal with both scenarios – an easy-to-open gate, and one you have to dismount for.

Be prepared

Before you venture out it's a good idea to make sure that your horse is proficient at turns about the forehand

and, ideally, turns on the haunches as well. Any good book on equitation will explain the aids and execution of these two movements; they are quite easy, besides which they are the forerunners of lateral movements, and help to make a horse manoeuvrable and obedient to the leg and rein.

The horse also needs to respond

reliably to the voice, and to stand still whilst you get on again, not to mention leading obediently in hand. The very act of working around gates will reinforce this behaviour, though.

It is sensible to practise the following techniques at home first so that all this is not entirely new to your horse when you are out alone, and struggling with a horse who finds gates worrying or confusing.

Gates that open from the saddle

Approach the gate towards the catch end: if the catch is on the right you will be using your left hand. Position your horse with his left (near) side sideways on to the gate so that you do not have to lean over too much, say 'stand', undo the catch and try to keep hold of the gate with your left hand, or push it open, as you bring your right hand left to the withers, so pressing on his neck with the right rein, and using your right leg on the girth. If you have both done your homework, the horse should do a sort of turn on the haunches towards the gate, preferably pushing it with his shoulder. Say whatever word he is trained to, such as 'over'.

When it is open far enough, ask for a turn about the forehand to the left (ie quarters stepping to the right), using your left leg behind the girth and, if feasible, at first keeping hold of the gate with your left hand to stabilize it. Once through and round the end of it, ask your horse for a turn on the haunches to the right (forehand moving right), ideally pushing the gate with his shoulder, or you can push the gate with your right hand. Ask him to stand while you fasten the catch. Praise him.

If it opens towards you, the same movements apply, but you will have to pull the gate open, go through, and then pull it shut, so the horse will also need to know about stepping backwards. This sounds extremely technical, but it is easier in practice.

Gates you need to dismount for

Approach the gate at the catch end (let's say right) and jump or slide off, according to your agility. Loop the reins with the buckle over your right arm, maybe cross the stirrups over the saddle, open the gate and lead your horse through, saying 'walk on'. He will automatically swing round on his forehand. Close and fasten the gate.

If you want to mount from the ground – though be aware that this is bad for your back, your horse's back and your saddle – position the horse with his right side against the gate to encourage him not to swing away, and tell him to stand as you mount.

If you do not want to mount from the ground, lead your horse with his near side against the gate and position him so that the saddle is next to the hinge end and say 'stand'. Climb halfway up the bars at that end and have your whip in the hand which may be holding the saddle either at the pommel or waist, not the cantle which can twist the tree. This is so that the whip will be on the side away from you to discourage him from moving that way. Also, have the rein furthest from you shorter than the other so that his head will be slightly away from you and if he does move, his quarters will come towards the gate. That way you will not be doing the splits in mid-air as you would if he moved the other way.

145

98 Vary work and exercise

One of the easiest ways to sour, sicken and sadden a horse is to keep doing the same work all the time. Unfortunately, many horses do not hack out these days because their riders are frightened of going on the roads, and facilities for other, more varied work, may be limited. Interestingly, most horses never get sick of hacking!

Why bother to vary work?

The reason for varying work is simply to keep the horse mentally fresh, stimulated, enthusiastic and happy. We ourselves may have to do the same kind of work day after day, but we understand the need for it and can push ourselves. Horses cannot do that, and many of them lead very boring lives, particularly in winter when turnout may be limited.

Horses that are generally kept

rigidly to one or two activities do take a little time to adapt to something different, but they soon enjoy it once they understand what is involved. I feel particularly sorry for horses who are stabled most or all of their time, whatever the season, brought out only to work in a schooling area and then put back in their boxes again. This must be a soul-destroying existence – but it is common in many professional and 'serious amateur' yards. I do not hold at all with the excuse that the horses are too valuable to risk on either

turning out or on other activities.

Whatever job a horse does, a change is as good as a rest because it is, actually, a mental rest. The greater variety of things a horse learns, the more his intelligence is challenged and comes to the fore, the steadier and more worldly wise he becomes, and the better a partner he will be.

Try these ideas

Many of us find it hard to think beyond what we normally do. We may also have the idea that because our horses are not used for certain activities, or have never done them, they won't behave well doing something different. This is not true. Many horses retire from one career and go on to something perhaps a little less demanding as they get older or suffer from injuries. Horses are very adaptable and naturally enquiring, and modern science is at last proving that they are capable of absorbing and acting on very much more education than we ever dreamed that they would be capable of.

Make use of poles, obstacles and hazards

Maybe you are the sort of rider who really doesn't want either to leave the ground – as in jumping – or to hit it – as in falling off – and there's nothing wrong with that; but that doesn't mean that you cannot use poles in different patterns either on the ground or raised just a few centimetres or inches.

Tellington TTEAM work is valuable for this (*see* Further Reading page 150), and particularly for scatty horses who

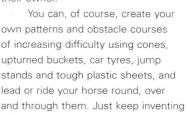

are not really 'connected' with their owners, as it really gets them thinking, problem solving and concentrating on their owner.

You can, of course, create your own patterns and obstacle courses of increasing difficulty using cones, upturned buckets, car tyres, jump stands and tough plastic sheets, and lead or ride your horse round, over and through them. Just keep inventing different ones to do.

Teach your horse to drive

There are several excellent books on driving for beginners, and it really is fun. Training vehicles are not that expensive, and neither is a basic harness. You can actually use your vehicle for transport! Take a friend shopping, and take it in turns to stay with the horse.

Farm park rides

One of the ways in which farms and estates are diversifying is by creating rides (with or without jumps) around their land. Depending on where your horse lives, you could either hack or box to your nearest one and make a day out of it, eating sandwiches whilst your horse grazes in hand between spells of work – or fun. Alternatively, you could try to persuade your own livery yard to create one, and hire it out.

Work to music

Get a decent battery-operated tape or CD player and have music playing in the background whilst you ride or do groundwork with your horse. Liberty work is particularly good fun, and really enhances your relationship with your horse. Concentrate first on getting him used to vocal aids and whip and body positions, and make liberal use of treats when he gets the smallest thing right. Then try simple movements at liberty, and build from there.

Under saddle

147

99 Warm up your horse before work

How can warming up before work affect a horse's behaviour? Apart from the physical necessity to get the blood flowing and give the muscles and other tissues the time and stimulus to gear up for more effort, a correct warm-up disciplines the horse's mind and makes him more comfortable, so helping to avoid evasive behaviour and injuries.

How to do it

Bring your horse into the manège at a relaxed walk on as loose a rein as you dare, ideally just holding the buckle, depending on whether or not he is prone to spooking. The horse needs to move very freely to keep his muscles alternately contracting and relaxing, which encourages blood flow through them. If muscles are held in more or less contraction all the time, this process is hampered.

Talk to your horse and use mainly your seat, legs and weight for direction, suggesting with your eyes and light rein aids that the head should be down and the horse should look into

his bends. The front of the face must not be behind the vertical. Look ahead to where you want to go, particularly round circles and bends, not down at your horse, which pressurizes him and, believe it or not, puts him on the forehand. Use the inside track and make different shapes in the manège; do not just go round and round the outside track.

Still on a loose rein, move up to a steady, long, loose, flowing trot after a good five minutes in walk, and use the same techniques and principles. Use your bodyweight and legs to keep him up off his forehand. If you lightly encourage the head down and, with your legs, the hindquarters and legs to

reach under and forwards, the horse will not fall on to the forehand and over-stress his forelegs.

Finally, do a long, lolloping canter on a loose rein in the same way – easy, relaxed and not fast. Be firm with your mind and voice to steady the horse, and do not let him fall in on the turns in an incorrect bend: correct this by sitting slightly to the outside with the outside leg slightly back, supporting with the inside leg and raising the inside hand a little or tapping it on the withers.

This process should take about ten minutes, though you should spend longer in cold weather when muscles can be stiff with cold. Do not forget to cool down after work.

100 Teach your horse to accept the whip

More and more horses seem to be whip shy these days, which makes me feel really sorry for them, and angry with their former riders. Beating a horse up never does any good, and is usually a sign of failure on the part of the trainer to get through to the horse, to discipline him in a more logical way, or to control his or her temper.

Why does my horse need to accept a whip?

Maybe he doesn't. If it makes your horse really unhappy and you don't have any problems with control or co-operation, then there is no need for it.

Whips can be useful to stress to a horse that you really *do* want him to obey your leg on that side for whatever reason, but the instant you touch some horses they either become so upset or angry that they will not co-operate anyway, or react violently.

A high-visibility whip, perhaps with a fluorescent tab or short ribbon tied on the end, is a useful way of asking traffic to keep clear of you.

How can I overcome this problem?

Horses have long and brilliant memories. They can 'unlearn' some things, but I have always found that getting frightened horses accustomed to a whip is a long, uncertain process. Trying desensitization techniques (*see* photos) may be helpful.

If you have a really good 'bond' with your horse, you may be able to start just carrying a whip, making sure that it never touches the horse or looks as though it is going to. Over time, the horse should come to realize that you do not use it even though other humans have. Remember, horses can see backwards, and can see your legs, sometimes your hands, and

certainly your whip. One suspicious incident, to the horse, or actual contact, can spoil your relationship for quite some time, if not permanently, once that trust has been broken. (Incidentally, I often find that horses do not regard my white TTEAM 'wand' in the same light as an ordinary, darker whip, so it may be worth giving this idea a try.)

If you have good control of your legs and feel that you need the whip because the horse is not listening to your leg aids, you may be better wearing blunt, rounded spurs.

Useful addresses and Further reading

UK

The Equine Behaviour Forum
Grove Cottage
Brinkley
Newmarket
Suffolk   CB8 OSF
(Kindly enclose s.a.e. if requiring
a written reply from this non-profit
organization.)
Tel: (01223) 836970
www.gla.ac.uk/External/EBF

Natural Horsemanship magazine
Vowley Farm
Bincknoll Lane
Wootton Bassett
Wiltshire   SN4 8QR
Tel: (01793) 852115
www.vowleyfarm.co.uk

Horse-Centred Training
c/o The Barn
Mankinholes
Todmorden
Lancashire   OL14 6HR
Tel: (01706) 839059
www.equinebehaviouralrescue.co.uk

Natural Horse Group
Stonefold Farm
Ilton
North Yorkshire   HG4 4LA
Tel: (01765) 685850
www.naturalhorsegroup.co.uk

The Classical Riding Club
Eden Hall
Kelso
Roxburghshire
Scotland   TD5 7QD
Fax: (01890) 830667
www.classicalriding.co.uk

The Equine Shiatsu Association
St Peter's Stud
Upper Beeding
West Sussex   BN44 3HP
Tel: (01903) 814860

TTEAM – Tellington Touch Equine
Awareness Method
TTEAM Centre
Tilley Farm
Farmborough
Bath
Somerset
Tel: (01761) 471128
www.ttouchtteam.co.uk

Intelligent Horsemanship
Lethornes
Lambourn
Berkshire   RG17 8QS
Tel: (01488) 71300
Fax: (01488) 73783
www.intelligenthorsemanship.co.uk

US

TTEAM US Office
PO Box 3793
Santa Fé
New Mexico 87501-3793

Equine Research Foundation
PO Box 1900
Aptos
California 95001
www.equineresearch.org

AUSTRALIA

Australian Equine Behaviour Centre
Clonbinane Road
Broadford
Victoria 3658
www.aebc.com.au

Further reading

Fraser, Andrew F. *The Behaviour
of the Horse* (CAB International,
1992)
Hannay, Pamela *Shiatsu With
Horses* (J.A. Allen, 1999)
Hogg, Abigail *The Horse Behaviour
Handbook* (David & Charles,
2004)
Larrigan, Tanya *New Sensations*

for Horse and Rider (J.A. Allen,
2000)
Kiley-Worthington, Marthe *The
Behaviour of Horses* (J.A. Allen,
1987)
Kiley-Worthington, Marthe *Equine
Welfare* (J.A. Allen, 1987)
Kiley-Worthington, Marthe *Educating
Equines* (Whittet Books, 2004)
McBane, Susan *Bodywork for
Horses* (Sportsmans Press, 2005)
McBane, Susan *How Your Horse
Works* (David & Charles, 1999)
McBane, Susan and Davis, Caroline
*Complementary Therapies for
Horse and Rider* (David & Charles,
2001)
Mills, Daniel and Nankervis, Kathryn
Equine Behaviour (Blackwell
Science, 1999)
Pelicano, Sgt. Rick *Bombproof Your
Horse* (J.A. Allen, 2004)
Rashid, Mark *Considering The Horse*
(Johnson Books, Boulder USA,
1993)
Schramm, Ulrik *The Undisciplined
Horse* (J.A. Allen, 2003)
Skipper, Lesley *Inside Your Horse's
Mind* (J.A. Allen, 1999)
Sutton, Amanda *The Injury Free
Horse* (David & Charles, 2001)
Tellington-Jones, Linda *Improve Your
Horse's Well-Being* (Kenilworth
Press, UK, 1999 and Trafalgar
Square Publishing, USA, 1999)
Townley, Audrey *The Natural Horse*
(Crowood Press, 2003)
Thorn, Percy F. *Humane Horse-
Training* (Hutchinson, 1949)
Williams, Moyra *Equine Psychology*
(J.A. Allen, 1976)
Williams, Moyra *Understanding
Nervousness in Horse and Rider*
(J.A. Allen, 1999)
Wright, Maurice *The Jeffery Method
of Horse Handling* (Privately
published in Australia, 1973 and
later editions)

Index

Index

PICTURE ACKNOWLEDGEMENTS

All photography by David Waters and Dan Tucker at Horsepix.co.uk except pages listed below.

    With its roots in horse country and staffed by horse people, Horsepix is a leading provider of high quality equestrian stock photography.

David & Charles/Susan McBane: pp 27, 67, 76, 77, 104, 108(right)
Sue Devereaux: p75
David & Charles/Bob Atkins: pp 95(top), 137, 146, 147, 149
David & Charles/Neil Hepworth: pp 140, 141

Illustrations on pp 72–3 by Maggie Raynor taken from *The Horse Behaviour Handbook* by Abigail Hogg (also published by David & Charles)